MONTRÉAL CANADIENS

HOCKEY TRIVIA QUIZ BOOK

DON WEEKES

GREYSTONE BOOKS
Douglas & McIntyre
Vancouver/Toronto

For the boys on "Hockey World": Ross Francoeur, Gerry Laderoute, Mosé Persico and two outstanding hosts, Rob Faulds and Dick Irvin.

Copyright © 1994 by Don Weekes

94 95 96 97 98   5 4 3 2 1

Greystone Books
A division of Douglas & McIntyre Ltd.
1615 Venables Street
Vancouver, British Columbia
V5L 2H1

The publisher gratefully acknowledges the assistance of the Canada Council and the British Columbia Ministry of Tourism, Small Business and Culture for its publishing programs.

Canadian Cataloguing in Publication Data

Weekes, Don
 Montreal Canadiens

"Greystone Books."
ISBN 1-55054-165-X
1. Montreal Canadiens (Hockey team)—Miscellanea. I. Title
GV848.M6W43 1994   796.962'64'0971428   C94-910451-5

Editing by Brian Scrivener
Jacket design by Eric Ansley & Associates Ltd.
Typesetting by Fiona MacGregor
Cover photo of Patrick Roy by Bruce Bennett/Bruce Bennett Studios
Printed and bound in Canada by Best Gagné Book Manufacturers, Inc.
Printed on acid-free paper [logo]

Don Weekes, *a Montréal television producer/writer with* CFCF *—* TV 12's *nationally syndicated sports magazine,* "Hockey World," *grew up playing hockey on the "back river" off Île Bigras, a small island suburb between Montréal and Laval. He watched his first Canadiens game at the Forum in 1958.*

CONTENTS

PREFACE

More than any other team, the Montréal Canadiens represent hockey tradition. From the earliest days, the winning spirit of player/manager combinations like Howie Morenz and Léo Dandurand or Patrick Roy and Ronald Corey have lifted the Canadiens beyond mere mortals to win more championships than any other team in professional sports, a fact well known and abundantly obvious on any trip to the Forum. But past the fabled 24 Stanley Cup banners, the Wall of Fame and the imposing murals of Maurice Richard, Jean Béliveau and Guy Lafleur lies the story of the legends whose exploits built and rebuilt the Canadiens, both on-ice and in the front office.

The early, inauspicious years were dotted with Stanley Cups, but not until Frank Selke and the Rocket produced the Canadiens' first dynasty powerhouse was the bleu-blanc-rouge tradition fully realized. The on-ice triumphs of the Flying Frenchmen and their brand of "firewagon hockey" filled their legions of fans with pride, even reverence. More than heroes, *les joueurs du Tricolore* became hockey deities; and for those "south of the border," the Canadiens, in their celebrated red uniforms with the famous "CH" crest, were always the team to beat.

Sam Pollock succeeded Selke, organizing two more dynasties before the 1970s were over. And since then, another two Cups have come home to Montréal. Consistency at all levels has been the Canadiens' hallmark. Today, former coaches and players, such as Bob Gainey, Pat Burns, Jacques Lemaire and Scotty Bowman, who soaked up the game under the Canadiens' system of disciplined two-way hockey, have graduated to run almost one-third of the NHL's 26 teams.

Through the years, others have benefitted, too. Ask the Oilers' Glen Sather what he picked up from playing as a Habs' journeyman and he'll tell you: "Winning." Or the powerful 1975 Soviet Red Army team that had never been so outplayed in any game as they were when they went up against the defensive corps of the Canadiens' Big Three.

It has been a history as diverse as any in sport; from the Rocket's fiftieth to little events like brother goalies Ken and Dave Dryden's handshake at centre ice after playing against each other, an NHL first.

This book marks many of those special occasions, some easily remembered, others more faint, like the memories of backyard hockey games on cold winter nights.

In writing this book, I would like to thank the Canadiens' Bernard Brisset for his support, researchers Liam McGuire and Allen Bishop for lending their expertise along the way and editor Brian Scrivener, graphic artist Ivor Tiltin and game designer Adrian van Vlaardingen.

I am indebted to a number of hockey writers and broadcasters, who helped make this book possible through their own work over many years, including Charles L. Coleman, Chrys Goyens, Allan Turowetz, Georges-Hébert Germain, Réjean Tremblay, Roy MacGregor, Herb Zurkowski, Red Fisher, Ron Reusch, Dick Irvin, Bill Beacon and Michael Farber.

Special thanks to Jean Béliveau, Dickie Moore, Dollard St. Laurent, Dave Dryden, Camil DesRoches, Doug Moore, Frédérique Cardinal, Frank Selke, Jr. and Sam Pollock.

DON WEEKES
June 1994

1

THE WARM-UP

Long gone are the days when players could "play themselves into shape." Today the basics of pre-season conditioning are well known and players train year round. In this warm-up quiz, we work out the cobwebs and build up your endurance on a variety of Canadiens' topics: scoring statistics, hockey history and unusual facts and anecdotes. If you're not "sucking wind" after a 40-second shift on these questions, you're ready for any one-on-one battle.

(Answers are on page 7)

1.1 **From which end of the Forum do the Canadiens always start each game?**
A. North
B. East
C. South
D. West

1.2 **Before the Canadiens settled on the famous "CH" crest another letter, instead of the "H", was used inside the large "C". Which letter?**
A. An "A"
B. A smaller "C"
C. A "M"
D. A "Q"

1.3 Who was the Canadiens' first million dollar-a-year player?
A. Guy Lafleur
B. Patrick Roy
C. Denis Savard
D. Vincent Damphousse

1.4 In what season did Guy Lafleur stop wearing his helmet?
A. 1971–72
B. 1972–73
C. 1973–74
D. 1974–75

1.5 Who was the only team to defeat the Canadiens at home during their best season ever, 1976–77?
A. The Philadelphia Flyers
B. The Boston Bruins
C. The New York Rangers
D. The Vancouver Canucks

1.6 Which Canadiens' defenseman is tied with Doug Harvey for most assists in one game?
A. Chris Chelios
B. Lyle Odelein
C. Larry Robinson
D. Guy Lapointe

1.7 Who was the last Canadiens' coach to regularly wear a hat behind the bench?
A. Dick Irvin
B. Claude Ruel
C. Babe Siebert
D. Toe Blake

1.8 What do Henri Richard, Jean-Guy Talbot, Bob Turner and Claude Provost all share in common?

A. All played their entire careers in Montréal.
B. Each won five Cups in his first five NHL seasons.
C. Each captained the Canadiens for at least one game.
D. Each scored Cup-winning goals for the Canadiens' 1956–60 dynasty team.

1.9 What Canadiens' trading card has the highest value?

A. Bernie Geoffrion, 1951–52, Parkhurst
B. Jacques Plante, 1955–56, Parkhurst
C. Maurice Richard, 1951–52, Parkhurst
D. Jean Béliveau, 1953–54, Parkhurst

1.10 What individual award did Bob Gainey win four consecutive times?

A. The Lester Patrick Trophy
B. The Bill Masterton Trophy
C. The Conn Smythe Trophy
D. The Frank J. Selke Trophy

1.11 Which Canadien inspired broadcaster Danny Gallivan to invent the expression "spinnerama?"

A. Serge Savard
B. Bobby Rousseau
C. Pete Mahovlich
D. Yvan Cournoyer

1.12 Which Bruin was the "extra man" when Boston got caught with too many men on the ice late in game seven of the 1979 semi-finals?
A. Mike Milbury
B. Jean Ratelle
C. Terry O'Reilly
D. Stan Jonathan

1.13 Which country produced the Canadiens' record-holder for most points in a season by a rookie?
A. United States
B. Sweden
C. Czechoslovakia
D. Canada

1.14 What was so special about Toe Blake's retirement gift?
A. It had Stanley Cup silver in it.
B. It was once owned by Canadiens great Howie Morenz.
C. It was donated to his favourite charity.
D. It was sealed in cement below centre ice at the Forum.

1.15 Which ex-Canadien Stanley Cup winner won another Stanley Cup while playing with another team, each win coming on Forum ice?
A. Rick Wamsley
B. Rob Ramage
C. Mark Hunter
D. Doug Risebrough

1.16 Which statement is incorrect?
A. Guy Lafleur wore No. 16 in his first All-Star game.
B. Bobby Orr wore No. 5 in his first All-Star game.
C. Jean Béliveau wore No. 14 in his first All-Star game.
D. Kirk Muller wore No. 17 in his first All-Star game.

1.17 Which Canadien ended the playing career of Scotty Bowman?
A. Marcel Bonin
B. Jean-Guy Talbot
C. Doug Harvey
D. Émile "Butch" Bouchard

1.18 Besides Ken Dryden which other Canadiens player(s) are the only NHLers ever to have won the Stanley Cup *prior* to capturing the Calder as top rookie?
A. Danny Grant
B. Guy Lafleur
C. Tony Esposito
D. Jacques Laperriere

1.19 Which Canadien became the first team captain by player *vote*?
A. Maurice Richard
B. Jean Béliveau
C. Bob Gainey
D. Guy Carbonneau/Chris Chelios

1.20 **What was veteran reporter Red Fisher's first NHL assignment covering the Canadiens?**
A. The Richard Riot
B. The signing of Jean Béliveau's first Canadiens contract
C. The firing of coach Dick Irvin
D. The resignation of referee Red Storey

1.21 **How many Stanley Cup rings does Canadiens' equipment manager Eddy Palchak own?**
A. At least four rings
B. Six rings
C. Eight rings
D. Ten or more rings

1.22 **Before Guy Lafleur, who was the last player to wear No. 10?**
A. Bill Collins
B. Ted Harris
C. Frank Mahovlich
D. Tom Johnson

1.23 **What is so special about Mario Tremblay's 1975–76 O–Pee–Chee rookie card?**
A. His rookie card has another player's NHL stats.
B. His card was short printed.
C. His card was printed mirror-image.
D. His card was mispictured.

1.24 **How much did the Canadiens sell their Montréal territorial rights for so that the Maroons could join the NHL?**
A. Nothing
B. $15,000
C. $150,000
D. $1,500,000

1.25 **What season was Patrick Roy playing the night he stopped the shot pictured on our front cover?**
A. 1991–92
B. 1992–93
C. 1993–94
D. 1994–95

THE WARM-UP
Answers

1.1 **A. North.**
The Canadiens have always started the first period from the north goal. It's a tradition that predates Frank Selke's arrival at the Forum in 1946, and by all accounts the original reason is unknown (except, perhaps, to the legendary ghosts of the Forum). What is known is that Selke standardized that ritual over the course of his 18-year term as GM, choosing south-end seats (Section One, Box Two), because he felt it was more advantageous to see his team's offense at work in front of the visitor's net twice, during the first and third periods.

1.2 **A. An "A."**

The Canadiens' famous "CH" logo has been a sports icon since 1917, when owner George Kennedy replaced the "A" (for Club Athlétique Canadien) inside the large

"C" with an "H" to symbolize the team's new name, Club de Hockey Canadien. Other than switching from bulky woollen knit to 100% polyester, the uniform's design and tri-colours have remained largely unchanged ever since.

1.3 C. Denis Savard.

Savard's four-year contract, at $1,087,500 U.S. per annum, made the former Chicago all-star centre an instant millionaire and the first million-dollar-a-year player in Canadiens' franchise history. The deal was struck in August 1990, two months before Roy's first million-a-year contract ($1,044,000) inked in October 1990. Savard's signing almost doubled his Blackhawk salary ($525,000 U.S.) after the trade that sent Chris Chelios to Chicago. Savard played three seasons (72–107–179) before being released to play in Tampa Bay.

1.4 D. 1974-75.

After three frustrating seasons of average play for the Québec favourite son who was supposed to become Jean Béliveau's successor and carry the Flying Frenchmen into the next dynasty, Lafleur forgot his helmet during 1974's training camp and metamorphosed into hockey's new phenom, le Démon Blond. For long-impatient Canadiens fans, the heir apparent had come. Lafleur, sans helmet, established his rightful place in Canadiens lineage of francophone superstars, leading Les Glorieux on to another string of Stanley Cups. With it came Lafleur's most enduring image: streaking down right wing, his blond mane trailing in his slipstream.

1.5   B. The Boston Bruins.

The Canadiens owned the NHL in 1976–77, establishing still-unbroken league records for most points (132 pts), most wins (60), most road wins (27), fewest losses (8) and fewest home losses (1). Their one Forum defeat came against Boston on October 30, 1976 in their sixth home game of the season. The winner was potted by Terry O'Reilly. Final score: 4–3. Scotty Bowman's Canadiens didn't lose again at home, establishing another NHL record for longest home undefeated streak (34 games).

1.6   B. Lyle Odelein.

A lot of players have stocked the Canadiens' blueline since Harvey set the NHL standard for defensive play 40 years ago, and Odelein may be the least likely Canadien defenseman to be recognized in any comparison, especially in an offensive category. Except for one night, and now, in one team record. On February 2, 1994 Odelein tied Harvey's 39-year-old record for five assists in one game. But unlike Harvey, Odelein collected "second assists" and didn't directly set up the scoring plays. No matter, the record stands and Odelein managed to class himself with the best.

1.7   D. Toe Blake.

When then-Canadiens coach Pat Burns stepped behind the Habs bench wearing a black fedora to celebrate the NHL's 75th anniversary at the 1992 season opener, he was honouring a sports tradition as venerable as the team playbook. The soft-felt fedora was standard attire for every coach, worn behind the bench, the front-office desk or on the train between games. Long after fashion (and most NHL coaches) abandoned the gentleman's hat, Toe Blake was still wearing his Biltmore at every game until his retirement in 1968.

1.8   B. Each won five Cups in his first five NHL seasons.

Richard, Talbot, Turner and Provost are the privileged rookies who made the Canadiens' camp in 1955 and held onto their player positions, successfully hoisting the Stanley Cup in five successive years, 1956 through 1960, next to veterans like Jean Béliveau, Doug Harvey and Maurice Richard.

1.9   C. Maurice Richard, 1951–52, Parkhurst.

Although the Rocket's career began in the 1940s, his rookie card wasn't issued until 1951–52, the year production of hockey cards began again after the Second World War. Today, the 1951–52 Parkhurst has a $2,000 U.S. value in mint condition. The next most valuable Canadiens cards are: Maurice Richard's 1952–53 Parkhurst ($1,000 U.S.), Jean Béliveau's 1953–54 Parkhurst ($750 U.S.), Jacques Plante's 1955–56 Parkhurst ($750 U.S.) and Bernie Geoffrion's 1951–52 Parkhurst ($400 U.S.)

1.10   D. The Frank J. Selke Trophy.

Working up and down the left wing for 16 years, Gainey was considered the NHL's best all-round, two-way player, excelling in every aspect of the game. Scoring key goals or forechecking and backchecking, Gainey defined the defensive forward position, for which he was awarded four straight Selke Trophies in its first four years. Perhaps the Canadiens winger's highest praise came from the usually stoic Soviet coach, Viktor Tikhonov, who viewed Gainey as "technically, the best player in the world today."

1.11 A. Serge Savard.
When Gallivan called play-by-play no word was out of bounds. And when the English language failed him, Gallivan made up new words and expressions like "Savardian spinnerama," inspired by Savard's classic 360 degree turn that sent the Habs defenseman spinning off a forechecking opponent.

1.12 B. Jean Ratelle.
It proved to be the turning point of the 1979 Stanley Cup playoffs. The Bruins, only minutes away from winning game seven in the semi-finals, are called for too many man on the ice after a poor line change. Jean Ratelle gets caught, giving the Canadiens a power play and Guy Lafleur's game-tying goal. In overtime, the Bruins go down and the Canadiens go on, soundly defeating the Rangers in the finals.

1.13 B. Sweden.
After all the Québec and Western Hockey League juniors the Canadiens have drafted, Europe was the last place the club expected to hawl in *two* record-holding rookie point-getters. Three years after Mats Naslund became the Canadiens' first Swede and the team's all-time leading point-earner among rookies with 71 points (26–45–71) in 1982–83, another Swedish star drafted by Montréal matched Naslund's record: 23-year-old Kjell Dahlin netted 71 points (32–39–71) in 1985-86. Not one, but two Swedes hold the Canadiens' record for most season-points by a rookie.

1.14 A. It had Stanley Cup silver in it.
The Club de Hockey Canadiens celebrated Toe Blake's long association with the team by presenting the 11-time Cup-winner with a silver bowl made in part from silver taken from the original Stanley Cup. How they'd get the famous sterling? Let's just say the Canadiens

were winning a lot of Cups in those years, and made good on their plans to honour Toe in a very special way.

1.15 B. Rob Ramage.
Since Calgary is the only team in Stanley Cup history to beat the Canadiens and win the Cup on Forum ice, the Canadien Cup-winner must have been a Flame champion, too. Ramage is the only player to win Cups at the Forum with two different teams, once with Calgary (1989) and, again, as a Canadien (1993). Risebrough, ex-Calgary coach and ex-Canadien, gets runner-up mention.

1.16 C. Jean Béliveau wore No. 14 in his first All-Star game.
In fact, in Béliveau's first All-Star match in 1954, the defending Stanley Cup champions still played against a roster of the NHL's best, and since the Canadiens were the previous year's Cup-winner he wore his own jersey, the Habs No. 4. Ever since the All-Star format changed in 1968 (conference vs. conference) players on both teams are assigned sweater numbers based on seniority. Rookie all-star Orr donned No. 5 and No. 2 in deference to Béliveau's No. 4 in 1968 and 1969; Lafleur wore No. 16 (Carol Vadnais had No. 10) in 1975 and ex-Devil Muller got No. 17 (Ron Francis had No. 9) in 1985. Just like most rookie all-stars, Béliveau was subjected to a number switch. In his second All-Star game, playing against the Cup-winning Red Wings, veteran Bill Gadsby used No. 4 and Béliveau No. 14.

1.17 B. Jean-Guy Talbot.
Bowman's on-ice career ended in 1951 after suffering a fractured skull as a result of a slash by Talbot. The Québec Junior League assessed a one-year suspension to the 19-year-old Talbot, but Bowman never played

another game, soon focussing his talents on coaching. Talbot played 12 seasons with the Canadiens and in his declining years made a comeback in St. Louis, hired by the same hockey man whose playing career he cut short, coach and manager of the Blues, Scotty Bowman.

1.18 A & C. Danny Grant and Tony Esposito.

In NHL history only three players have ever won the Cup before the Calder—and all three played with the Habs. Dryden is best known for bringing down the Bruins and the Blackhawks in the 1971 Cup playoffs and winning top rookie the following season; but so did Grant and Esposito who won rings with Montréal in 1968 and 1969 respectively and then took NHL rookie honours the next year with other teams. Grant produced a solid first season in Minnesota with 34 goals and 65 points in 75 games. Tony O's play was spectacular, recording 15 shutouts (2.17 GAA) with Chicago in 1969-70. Neither player ever won the Cup again, but both proved their value and how tough it was to crack the Canadiens lineup, a team with the same three centres—Jean Béliveau, Ralph Backstrom and Henri Richard—for 14 years during the 1950s and 60s.

1.19 B. Jean Béliveau.

Traditionally, team captains are chosen by the players, most often awarded by consensus and seniority. But Béliveau's captaincy in 1961 was the first decided by player vote and one which ultimately required two ballots to settle. The first ballot produced a four-way tie between veterans Bernie Geoffrion, Dickie Moore, Tom Johnson and big Jean; in the second round the majority of the players voted for Béliveau, much to Geoffrion's dissatisfaction.

1.20 A. The Richard Riot.

No one has covered the Canadiens longer than Fisher.
And few reporters can boost of a more eventful intro-
duction to the NHL than Fisher's first assignment on
March 17, 1955—the night of the Richard Riot. The
Montréal Star's rookie reporter survived an egg pelting,
tear-gas and the violent mob scene outside the Forum.
After that career debut, his next 40 years in sports were
almost a cake walk.

1.21 D. Ten or more rings.

Since joining the Canadiens as equipment manager
(then called trainer) in 1966, Palchak has been on 10
Cup winners between 1968 and 1993. Palchuk's ring
collection equals the number won by Gordie Howe,
Wayne Gretzky and Mario Lemieux combined. No
other non-player has had his name engraved on the
Cup more often than Palchak.

1.22 C. Frank Mahovlich.

In every game of his 18-year NHL career, Mahovlich
wore his favourite No. 27 . . . except for one game: his
first as a Canadien. Only 24 hours after being traded,
the "Big M" joined the team in Minnesota. But his No.
27 wasn't available (since no Canadien had ever worn
that number), so Mahovlich slipped on No. 10 for the
game, January 14, 1971. No one used No. 10 again until
Lafleur made his debut in October 1971.

1.23 D. His card was mispictured.

When O–Pee–Chee printed Tremblay's 1975–76 rookie
card they used the mug of Gord McTavish of the
Sudbury Wolves. Both rookies were first-round draft
picks by Montréal in 1974 (Tremblay was 12th,
McTavish 15th overall) but while Tremblay soared,
McTavish fizzled, never making the NHL. The
McTremblay card is worth $3.00, six times more than
other cards in that set.

1.24 B. $15,000.

Yes, the $15,000 price tag for an NHL franchise was insignificant, even by 1924 standards, but it wasn't charity Canadiens owner Léo Dandurand was offering when he allowed the Maroons into Montréal. His motive was to profit from Montréal's distinctive English and French communities. Dandurand, the consummate promoter, gave Montréalers two hockey teams to call their own and for 14 years (1924-38) it worked, stirring a natural rivalry both on and off the ice.

1.25 B. 1992–93.

It seemed fitting that on the 100th anniversary of the Stanley Cup, the game's best player, Wayne Gretzky, should be challenging hockey's greatest dynasty franchise, the 23-time Cup-winning Canadiens. And what better representative to celebrate the league's centennial (and our cover), than its top netminder and Conn Smythe Trophy winner, Patrick Roy, who gets captured in this riveting moment during the 1993 playoff finals. A trained hockey eye could tell that our Roy shot happened sometime in 1992-93, the only season he wore the NHL's centennial crest (on the lower right shoulder). So how do we know the photo comes from the Canadiens' 24th Cup drive? Trust us. It happened in overtime in game four, June 7, 1993.

SWEATER NUMBERS

The Canadiens have handed out jersey numbers from 0 to 99 in their 85-year history. Match the most recognizable Canadiens and their famous jersey numbers.

(Solution is on page 116)

Patrick Roy
Steve Shutt
Frank Mahovlich
Bobby Rousseau
Bob Gainey
Howie Morenz
Ken Dryden
Guy Lapointe
John LeClair
Henri Richard/Elmer Lach
Jean Béliveau/Aurèle Joliat

Chris Chelios
Mats Naslund
Doug Harvey
Kirk Muller
Claude Provost
Dick Duff
Jacques Lemaire
Pete Mahovlich
Pierre Larouche

Maurice Richard
Jacques Plante
Émile Bouchard
Serge Savard
Yvan Cournoyer
Guy Carbonneau
Larry Robinson
Ralph Backstrom
Guy Lafleur
Lorne Worsley

No. 1 _____
No. 2 _____
No. 3 _____
No. 4 _____
No. 5 _____
No. 6 _____
No. 7 _____
No. 8 _____
No. 9 _____
No. 10 _____
No. 11 _____
No. 12 _____
No. 14 _____
No. 15 _____
No. 16 _____

No. 17 _____
No. 18 _____
No. 19 _____
No. 20 _____
No. 21 _____
No. 22 _____
No. 23 _____
No. 24 _____
No. 25 _____
No. 26 _____
No. 27 _____
No. 28 _____
No. 29 _____
No. 30 _____
No. 33 _____

2

NICKNAMES AND
LESSER-KNOWN LEGENDS

Serge Savard, Guy Lapointe and Larry Robinson are well known as the Canadiens' "Big Three," but who played on the "Doughnut Line," where was "Alcatraz" and how did "Toe" Blake come by his nickname? Here's a look at some familiar aliases and not-so-recognizable characters in Canadiens' history.

(Answers are on page 20)

2.1   Who nicknamed Maurice Richard, "The Rocket?"
   A. A teammate
   B. A fan
   C. A coach
   D. A reporter

2.2   Who played on the Canadiens' "Doughnut Line?"
   A. Henri Richard and Maurice Richard
   B. Jean Béliveau and Bernie Geoffrion
   C. Guy Lafleur and Steve Shutt
   D. Vincent Damphousse and Brian Bellows

2.3   What hotel became known as "Alcatraz" to the Canadiens in 1986?
   A. Le Méridien Montréal
   B. Sheraton Île Charron
   C. Hotel Château Versailles
   D. Château Bromont

2.4 Who is Malcolm Campbell?
A. The minister at Howie Morenz's funeral
B. The first anglophone on the Canadiens
C. The Canadiens' first American-born player
D. The Forum's first national anthem singer

2.5 When did Hector Blake pick up his nickname, "Toe"?
A. Before his hockey career began
B. While playing city league hockey
C. While playing with the Maroons
D. While with the Canadiens

2.6 Who were the so-called "Three Musketeers" in Canadiens' history?
A. The Forum's in-house officiating staff
B. A Montréal Maroons' scoring line
C. Three early owners of the Canadiens
D. A trio of Montréal radio announcers on the Hot Stove League

2.7 Who is Eddie Litzenberger?
A. The Canadiens' equipment manager
B. A Calder rookie-winner given away by the Canadiens
C. The Canadiens' first NHL rookie of the year
D. The first German-born player on the Canadiens

2.8 Which Canadien was nicknamed "Joe" for his hard work forechecking on the 1956–60 dynasty team?
A. Phil Goyette
B. Marcel Bonin
C. Claude Provost
D. Donnie Marshall

2.9 **Which Canadien did Leaf coach Punch Imlach call a "Junior B goalie?"**
A. Rogie Vachon
B. Michel Larocque
C. Phil Myre
D. Michel Plasse

2.10 **Who is Joe Schaefer?**
A. The pennant hanger at the Forum
B. The first Canadien awarded a penalty shot
C. A little-used Rangers' backup goalie
D. The Canadiens' first non-francophone coach

2.11 **Who are the "Black Aces?"**
A. A doo-whoop group of national anthem singers
B. Any benched rookies
C. Any unfair official
D. Jean Béliveau's last semi-pro team before joining the Canadiens

2.12 **From where was Jean Béliveau's nickname "Le Gros Bill" derived?**
A. A 19th-century hockey legend
B. A traditional folk song
C. An early radio drama
D. A religious parable

2.13 **Who did the press call "The Twelve Apostles?"**
A. The 12 Stanley Cup-winning Canadiens coaches
B. The first 12 Canadiens in the Hall of Fame
C. The only 12 five-time members of the NHL's first All-Star team
D. The 12 players from the 1956–60 dynasty team

NICKNAMES AND
LESSER-KNOWN LEGENDS
Answers

2.1. A. A teammate.

Although many Montréal reporters claim they nick-named Richard, teammates began using "The Rocket" in the dressing room long before the press turned it into public domain. Canadiens' forward Ray Getliffe was first to observe at an early Richard practice: "That kid can take off just like a rocket." A few nights later, Getliffe all but carved it into the Forum's foundation by saying, "There he goes again, just like a rocket." The nickname stuck and Richard was for evermore hockey's "Rocket."

2.2 C. Guy Lafleur and Steve Shutt.

It was Pierre Bouchard who coined Lafleur and Shutt's scoring line, the "Doughnut Line," because the two wingers played with "a hole in the centre," first filled by Henri Richard, then Pete Mahovlich and, finally, Jacques Lemaire.

2.3 B. Sheraton Île Charron.

In their playoff bid for their 23rd Stanley Cup, the Canadiens settled into segregated residence off-Montréal island at the Sheraton Hotel on Île Charron. Known among the players as "Alcatraz" (after the famous island prison in San Francisco Bay), the island retreat became a two-month sentence, isolating the players from their wives, girlfriends and the press corps. As the playoffs advanced, their home-away-from-home kept out distractions and drew veterans and rookies closer together, a small sacrifice for the privilege of winning the Stanley Cup.

2.4   A. The minister at Howie Morenz's funeral.
From early morning to mid-afternoon on March 11,
1937 fans filled the Forum to pay their respects to the
Canadiens first superstar, Howie Morenz. His body lay
instate at centre ice with his teammates forming a
guard of honour as Reverend Malcolm Campbell deliv-
ered the service. Outside, thousands lined the streets
two and three people deep to view the cortège as it
made its way from Atwater and St. Catherine to Côte
des Neiges Cemetery. Morenz is one of very few so
honoured at the Montréal Forum.

2.5   A. Before his hockey career began.
Blake's younger brother could not pronounce Hector; it
came out as "Hek–toe." Boyhood chums picked up on
it and "Toe" has been Blake's handle ever since.

2.6   C. Three early owners of the Canadiens.
Léo Dandurand, Joe Cattarinich and Louis Letourneau,
popularly known in Montréal during the 1920s as the
"Three Musketeers," purchased the Canadiens in a bid-
ding war for $11,000 and turned their Flying
Frenchmen into a solid team of skilled players that produced the NHL's first brand of "firewagon hockey."
The "Three Musketeers" under Dandurand managed
the club until 1935.

**2.7   B. A Calder rookie-winner given away by the
Canadiens.**
Among the many players NHL teams handed over to
shore up Chicago's fading franchise in the 1950s, the
Canadiens yielded Eddie Litzenberger, a bright
prospect from Saskatchewan. But unlike some of the
other castoffs, Litzenberger proved to be just what
Chicago needed to restore attendance and lift the club
out of the cellar. In the same season Montréal passed up
the right winger, the Hawks turned him into the NHL's

rookie of the year. Revenge was his again in 1961 when Chicago bumped off the Canadiens in the semi-finals and won the Cup.

2.8.　C. Claude Provost.

Best known as the only non-Hall of Famer who can claim nine Stanley Cup rings, Provost was indispensible as the grinding defensive forward, shadowing the Howes and Hulls so that the Béliveaus and Richards could score goals. Without much notice or praise, "Joe" became one of the Canadiens' true unsung heros.

2.9　A. Rogie Vachon.

Imlach's notorious sense of the dramatic was working overtime when his over-the-hill gang of Maple Leafs faced the heavily-favoured Canadiens in Expo year, 1967. Rookie Vachon weathered Imlach's publicity posturing but Toronto rained on Montréal's centennial parade by winning the Stanley Cup. Later, the "Junior B goalie" proved himself an NHL equal en route to Cups in 1968 and 1969.

2.10　C. A little-used Rangers' backup goalie.

On that fateful night in 1959 when Jacques Plante revolutionized the NHL by donning hockey's first goalie mask, Joe Schaefer was a no-name backup netminder. Yet today he figures prominently in the backroom strategizing that landed Plante between the pipes wearing his crude face protector with slits for the eyes and mouth. The opposing netminder that night was the Rangers' legendary Emile "the Cat" Francis. It's one of his favourite hockey stories. "After Bathgate's backhand forced Plante into the Garden's medic room for stitching, Jacques gave coach Toe Blake two options: play me with my mask or get yourself a backup," recalls Francis. "In those days the home team supplied both teams with the spare goalie, and in New York, it was Joe Schaefer. Earlier, Joe had played for Chicago and he let in nine goals in 18 minutes. After the game the press boys say: 'Was it a thrill to play tonight?' And Joe says, 'Oh yea.' They ask: 'What's your weakness?' Joe says: 'Shots!' Well, Toe knew Schaefer's reputation for soft goals. So when Plante refused to play without his mask, Toe's choice was obvious. Plante wore his mask. I couldn't believe it."

2.11 B. Any benched rookies.
Before a rookie makes regular rotation, he might spend time as a "Black Ace," watching games from the pressbox to learn about hockey systems. Steve Shutt is a classic Canadiens example. He followed many games from the pressbox in his first two seasons.

2.12 B. A traditional folk song.
Béliveau's 6' 3", 205-pound frame reminded Québec Aces fans (who first witnessed the big centre's end-to-end rushes) of the original "Gros Bill," an early-day superhero in the Paul Bunyan mould, made famous in the Québecois folksong, "Là Voilà Gros Bill" and featured in a 1950 film starring French actress Juliette Béliveau (no relation).

2.13 D. The 12 players from the 1956–60 dynasty team.
The "12 Apostles" inherited the glory and soul of the Canadiens and turned winning the Stanley Cup into a spring rite for an NHL record five consecutive seasons. The only Canadiens to play on all five championships were: Maurice Richard, Jean Béliveau, Jacques Plante, Dickie Moore, Claude Provost, Doug Harvey, Jean-Guy Talbot, Donnie Marshall, Bernie Geoffrion, Tom Johnson, Bob Turner and Henri Richard.

Across

1. 1 & 3 down: Goalie in picture
4. ____ Ross Trophy
5. ____ Carbonneau
6. Shot not on goal
7. "_____ top."
8. Other 1970 pro league (abbrev.)
9. "_____ the lead out."
11. _____-Star game
12. "The puck has _____"
14. Lyle _____
19. Claude _____
20. Ahead a goal, "have the ____."
22 & 49: Sang "O Canada" at Forum
24. Legendary goalie
26. _____ Cournoyer
27. "_____ the puck in."
29. "_____ into the boards."
30 & 8 down: 1980s goalie
31. Rink equipment
32. "_____ shoots, _____ scores."
33. "The siren _____ the period."
34. "_____ at the puck."
38. "_____ down the pace."
40. Russian goalie
42. Keith _____
45. Liquid ice
46. "Feed a _____"
48. Shayne _____
49. See 22 across
50. "_____ out the game."

Down

1. Mike _____
2. _____ Hockey League
3. See 1 across
5. Bob _____
7. Ontario junior league (abbrev.)
8. See 30 across
9. Paraphernalia
10. Electronic medium
13. Serge _____
15. Gatorade
16. Maple _____
17. 1940s coach
18. "_____ goal."
21. _____ Savard
23. Essence
25. Emblem on sweater
28. "_____ performance"
29. Crest letters
33. _____ Desjardins
34. Serge's other playing team
35. Gobbled up or ____ the puck
36. The Big _____
37. "Tale of the _____"
39. Defeat
40. _____-man advantage
41. "_____ out of time."
43. "_____'s meow."
44. Media relations (abbrev.)
47. Overtime

CROSSWORD: THE HABS

(Solution is on page 116)

3

LOOKING FOR MR. RIGHT

The Canadiens have always preferred to build from within their organization as opposed to making trades or acquiring free agents. The famous "C" form, which gave away a player's rights for life, was the lifeblood of Frank Selke's farm system before the amateur draft did away with sponsorship lists and NHL team-owned junior clubs. Pulled down by parity and victimized by their own success, the Canadiens wisely began swapping good players for future picks in order to replenish their talent pool. In this chapter we test your cunning to size up the top prospects and draft or trade accordingly.

Answers are on page 30)

3.1 **Who did Sam Pollock draft instead of Mike Bossy in 1977?**
   A. Doug Wickenheiser
   B. George Goulakos
   C. Mark Napier
   D. Danny Geoffrion

3.2 **Which Canadien was first traded away because of union activities for the players' association in 1957?**
   A. Ab McDonald
   B. Dollard St. Laurent
   C. Bert Olmstead
   D. Doug Harvey

3.3 Besides Petr Svoboda, who is the only other European chosen first in a draft by the Canadiens?
A. Oleg Petrov
B. Saku Koivu
C. Peter Popovic
D. Jyrki Lumme

3.4 Who was the highest draft pick for a goaltender in Canadiens' history?
A. Michel Larocque
B. Ray Martiniuk
C. Patrick Roy
D. Michel Plasse

3.5 What NHL club traded its first-round pick, allowing Montréal to choose Guy Lafleur in 1971?
A. The Oakland Seals
B. The Minnesota North Stars
C. The St. Louis Blues
D. The Los Angeles Kings

3.6 What draft year yielded the most Stanley Cups from players chosen in a first round?
A. 1971
B. 1972
C. 1974
D. 1975

3.7 Who or what did the Winnipeg Jets receive in the deal that brought Serge Savard back to the Canadiens in 1983?
A. Future considerations (1986's fourth-round choice)
B. $50,000 and a third-round choice
C. Robert Picard and a third-round choice
D. Savard was released without compensation.

3.8 Among the 27 players with the Canadiens on five championship teams from 1956 to 1960, how many were acquired through player trades?
A. Two players
B. Four players
C. Six players
D. Eight players

3.9 Who did the Canadiens trade away in 1970 to acquire the future draft spot in which Larry Robinson was chosen?
A. Ernie Hicke
B. Dick Duff
C. Fran Huck
D. Ralph Backstrom

3.10 What do Pierre Larouche, Peter Marsh, Peter Lee and Pete Mahovlich all share in common?
A. They were all traded together.
B. They were all traded for future draft picks.
C. They were all acquired 24 hours before trading deadline.
D. They all went unsigned as juniors.

3.11 Which NHL coach was not drafted by the Canadiens?
A. The Devils' Jacques Lemaire
B. The Kings' Barry Melrose
C. The Stars' Bob Gainey
D. The Sharks' Kevin Constantine

3.12 Which statement is incorrect?
   A. Jacques Laperriere was only the second defenseman to win the Calder as rookie of the year.
   B. The Punch Line (Lach, Richard and Blake) was not the first line to finish 1–2–3 in the NHL scoring race.
   C. Jean Béliveau never played against the Russians.
   D. Pete Mahovlich did not come to the Canadiens before brother Frank.

3.13 Which ex-Canadien made a comeback in the NHL after playing professional roller hockey?
   A. Rick Chartraw
   B. Yvan Cournoyer
   C. Jocelyn Lemieux
   D. José Charbonneau

3.14 How did the Canadiens acquire the services of Jean Béliveau in 1953?
   A. They bought a semi-pro hockey league.
   B. They traded away the future rights to two Québec junior prospects.
   C. They filed a court order against a junior team owner.
   D. They signed a secret agreement with his coach, Punch Imlach.

3.15 Which NHL team traded away its draft rights which led to the Canadiens choosing Patrick Roy?
   A. The Québec Nordiques
   B. The St. Louis Blues
   C. The Winnipeg Jets
   D. The Los Angeles Kings

3.16 **How many scouts work in the Canadiens organization?**
A. Six
B. 12
C. 15
D. 18

LOOKING FOR MR. RIGHT
Answers

3.1 **C. Mark Napier.**
In an uncharacteristic blunder for the master guru of the NHL draft, Sam Pollock heeded the advice of his chief scouts and let a Québec junior named Mike Bossy slip away because the young francophone sniper, according to scouting reports, lacked "courage" in the fight-filled Québec Junior League. As if! Instead, Toronto-born WHA star Napier got picked and immediately flamed out on the Canadiens, before producing respectable numbers in subsequent years. But nothing short of a superstar performance would save face or make up for losing the Lavalois kid who helped turn the Islanders into a dynasty.

3.2 **B. Dollard St. Laurent.**
Although it was Doug Harvey and Detroit's Ted Lindsay who led the first ill-fated NHL players' association in 1957, others like Dollard St. Laurent actively supported the fledging union, attending meetings and recruiting players. Despite losing their bid for recognition in 1957–58, the NHLPA made some gains. But it was at the expense of many hockey careers, including

St. Laurent's, who was soon dealt to Chicago, a team perpetually mired in the NHL's cellar. St. Laurent had good company, though. Lindsay, Detroit's Al Arbour and the Leafs' Tod Sloan all became Hawks as punishment for their union efforts. The Habs' Bert Olmstead, another union supporter, was dealt to Toronto that same year; Harvey wasn't moved until 1961, after the Canadiens lost their bid for a sixth straight Cup.

3.3   B. Saku Koivu.

The Canadiens have only ever picked two Europeans first in a draft, Svoboda (1984) and Finnish-born centre Koivu, who went 21st overall in 1993. The only other Canadiens' first-round European was Swede Jan Ingman, chosen 19th (third pick) in 1981.

3.4   D. Michel Plasse.

He's not only the Canadiens highest goalie pick, no other netminder in NHL history except Plasse has ever been drafted first overall. But that lofty status in 1968 couldn't save him after two average seasons with the Canadiens, who released him to Kansas City in the 1974 expansion draft. From there the NHL's only number-one-drafted goalie stopped for coffee in Pittsburgh, Colorado and Québec before retiring in 1982 with a 3.79 average in 299 games. The Canadiens' next highest goalie picks have been: Martiniuk, 5th overall in 1970 (a bust in the NHL), Michel Larocque, 6th overall in 1972 and Roy, 51st overall in 1984.

3.5   A. The Oakland Seals.

In 1967, GM Sam Pollock proposed league measures barring teams from foolishly trading future draft positions for veterans with immediate skills. The NHL nixed Pollock's idea and three years later the Canadiens, owners of four Cups in six seasons, secured 1971's premiere draft spot. The heist was easy for

Pollock (who traded Ernie Hicke and the Canadiens' 1970 first pick to Oakland for François Lacombe and the Seals first pick in 1971) until last place Oakland found their wheels and edged ahead of the faltering Kings. So Trader Sam sent Ralph Backstrom to Los Angeles and stalled Oakland's drive. The Seals finished last according to Pollock's plan and the Canadiens chose first, picking Oakland's pockets of the NHL's next superstar, Guy Lafleur.

3.6   C. 1974.
The Canadiens chose five times in 1974's first round, drafting four players who went on to win a combined 14 Stanley Cups. It was the most successful first round in draft history. The players were: Cam Conner (fifth pick overall, one Cup), Doug Risebrough (seventh, four Cups), Rick Chartraw (10th, four Cups) and Mario Tremblay (12th, five Cups).

3.7   B. $50,000 and a third-round choice.
After dismissing Irving Grundman, Ronald Corey looked over the best candidates for managing director and choose Savard, who was still a Jet with a one-year option. A little late-season negotiating with Winnipeg GM John Ferguson and Corey had Savard homeward bound in time for the 1983 entry draft. What did the Canadiens get when they originally traded Savard to the Jets in 1981? A sixth round draft pick (Ernie Vargas).

3.8   A. Two players.
Frank Selke's farm system was such a phenomenon that when the Canadiens won five straight Cups only two of 27 players from those teams were acquired in trades: Bert Olmstead (from Chicago) and Marcel Bonin (from Boston/Detroit). Selke's network across Canada sponsored feeder leagues to "beat the bushes" and supply

the Canadiens with "Québec flash and Prairie brawn," a team chemistry manifested in rookies like Henri Richard and Bob Turner. Seldom did another NHL team find a player not already known by the Canadiens; more often the other five clubs purchased from Selke's system.

3.9   B. Dick Duff.

In a rich draft year like 1971 (Guy Lafleur, Marcel Dionne and Rick Martin), Robinson went relatively late, second round, 20th overall. Never mind the other 13 teams who missed grabbing the Big Bird, the Canadiens only got to him on their fourth pick, behind Lafleur (obviously), Chuck Arnason (who?) and Murray Wilson (no way!). Veteran Canadien Dick Duff was the trade bait in 1970 that hooked Los Angeles into passing up its second-round pick (20th overall) and giving Montréal 17 years of Larry Robinson.

3.10   A. They were all traded together.

It was known as the "all Peter" deal. On November 29, 1977, Pittsburgh's Larouche and Marsh were dealt to Montréal for Mahovlich and Lee. Four Peters. The Canadiens got a 50-goal season from Larouche (1979-80) and nothing from Marsh (who stayed in the WHA), while the Penguins kept Mahovlich for two years and rookie Lee for six seasons and 431 games (114-131-245). Call the trade a draw. Interestingly, when Larouche moved to Hartford another Peter was involved, future draft pick Petr Svoboda.

3.11   A. The Devils' Jacques Lemaire.

The Canadiens may be the most successful team to draft future NHL coaches. Consider Gainey (1973), Melrose (1976) and Constantine (1978). Or Larry Robinson (1971), Steve Shutt (1972) or Doug Risebrough (1974). But Lemaire was never drafted; his status with the Junior Canadiens prevented his eligibility for selection in 1967. At the time any amateur player, 17 years and older, on an NHL-sponsored junior team or on sponsorship lists was ineligible for claim in the draft.

3.12 D. Pete Mahovlich did not come to the Canadiens before brother Frank.

In fact, Pete preceded Frank by 18 months. For the record, both brothers were acquired in Detroit trades; the younger Mahovlich arrived June 6, 1969 from the Wings with Bart Crashley for Garry Monahan and Doug Piper; and brother Frank, on January 13, 1971 for Mickey Redmond, Guy Charron and Bill Collins.

3.13 D. José Charbonneau.

Charbonneau, a Québec boy put through the media ringer after being chosen the Canadiens' number-one draft pick in 1985, had his NHL career resuscitated in 1993 thanks to a summer season of roller hockey with the Vancouver VooDoo. While VooDoo coach Tiger Williams deserves the credit for peddling Charbonneau to Canuck's GM Pat Quinn, it was the 25-year-old's work ethic and attitude which brought him back into the NHL. In 1993-94, injuries limited his play to 30 Canuck games and 14 points.

3.14 A. They bought a semi-pro hockey league.

The Canadiens spent three frustrating years trying to sign Béliveau away from the Québec Aces of the semi-professional Québec Senior Hockey League. On his two Canadiens tryouts (1951 and 1952) Gros Bill exhibited the qualities of a superstar-in-waiting. Finesse. Size. Spirit. And a heavy shot that goalies said felt like catching a brick. But his heart was still in Québec with the Aces fans who set attendance records (even by NHL standards) at Le Colisée, known today as "The house that Jean built." To sign the big centre, the Canadiens, who owned his pro rights by territorial jurisdiction, bought the entire Québec league and turned it professional, thereby altering Béliveau's player status, too. His contract called for $110,000 with bonuses, guarantees and other clauses that led to the inevitable question, "What convinced the Québec star to sign?" At the press conference in 1953, Frank Selke quipped: "It was really simple. All I did was open the Forum vault and say, 'Help yourself, Jean.' "

3.15 C. The Winnipeg Jets.

1984 was one of the Canadiens' strongest years at the draft. They switched first-round picks with Hartford and landed Petr Svoboda (fifth); then choose Shayne Corson (eighth) and Stéphane Richer (29th) before taking Patrick Roy 51st overall, a draft position the Canadiens picked up in 1983 when they sent defenseman Robert Picard to Winnipeg.

3.16 D. 18.

The Canadiens spend more than $1 million annually and employ 11 full-time and 7 part-time scouts in North America and Europe to identify the best prospects in junior, college and the pro ranks.

PAST AND FUTURE CONSIDERATIONS

Contrary to popular belief, except for a handful of untouch-
ables, few members of the Canadiens have been safe from the
trade. Even the greats, like Howie Morenz, Jacques Plante and
Doug Harvey, were put on the blocks for players, cash, draft
picks or even future considerations. Many of the best retired
untraded, others were released as free agents.

Match the traded players in the left and right columns.

(Solution is on page 117)

1. Stéphane Richer &   *FOR???*   A. Frank Eddolls &
   Tom Chorske   Joe Benoit
2. Doug Harvey   B. Bobby Smith
3. Mark Napier &   C. Ryan Walter &
   Keith Acton   Rick Green
4. Chris Chelios   D. Released/free agent
5. Howie Morenz   E. Aurèle Joliat
6. Ted Kennedy   F. Sylvain Turgeon
7. Shayne Corson,   G. Roger Jenkins &
   Brent Gilchrist &   Leroy Goldsworthy
   Vladimir Vujtek   H. Lou Fontinato
8. Larry Robinson   I. Denis Savard
9. Jacques Plante,   J. Kirk Muller &
   Phil Goyette &   Rolie Melanson
   Donnie Marshall   K. Vincent Damphousse
10. Newsy Lalonde   L. Gump Worsley, Dave
11. Claude Lemieux   Balon, Len Ronson &
12. Rod Langway, Brian   Léon Rochefort
    Engblom, Doug Jarvis &
    Craig Laughlin

4

JAKE THE SNAKE, ST. PATRICK AND OTHER GOALIE GREATS

Before every game Patrick Roy follows the same ritual. About 30 feet out, he crouches and stares at his posts, willing the goal to be smaller. Then he launches himself at his net, veering away at the last moment to circle the right and left corners before settling into his crease. From Georges Vézina to St. Patrick, Canadiens fans have always been treated to exceptional goaltending, as well as to some remarkable records and anecdotes.

(Answers are on page 41)

4.1 **Which Canadiens' goalie has the most wins in a season?**
A. Ken Dryden
B. George Hainsworth
C. Patrick Roy
D. Jacques Plante

4.2 **What NHL-first did Canadiens' netminder Georges Vézina accomplish?**
A. The NHL's first overtime win
B. The NHL's first goalie skates
C. The NHL's first-ever shutout
D. The NHL's first assist by a goalie

4.3 Who did Patrick Roy wink at during a stoppage in play in the 1993 Stanley Cup finals?
A. A Los Angeles King
B. A fellow Canadien
C. Goaltending coach François Allaire
D. A goal judge at the Forum

4.4 How many times did brothers Ken and Dave Dryden play opposite each other in nets?
A. Only once
B. Twice
C. Three times
D. More than five times

4.5 Which ex-Canadiens' goalie did Guy Lafleur score three 50th goals against?
A. Rogie Vachon
B. Denis Herron
C. Tony Esposito
D. Cesare Maniago

4.6 Which Canadiens' goalie holds the modern-day NHL record for longest shutout sequence?
A. Bill Durnan
B. Jacques Plante
C. Georges Vézina
D. Ken Dryden

4.7 Which Canadiens' goalie starred in the only shutout in All-Star game history?
A. Jacques Plante
B. Lorne Worsley
C. Charlie Hodge
D. Gerry McNeil

4.8 Ken Dryden played in only six regular season games before his famous playoff run of 1971. How many of those games did he lose?
A. None
B. Only one
C. Two
D. Two losses and two ties

4.9 Which goalie has recorded the most shutouts in Canadiens' history?
A. Ken Dryden
B. Patrick Roy
C. Jacques Plante
D. George Hainsworth

4.10 When was the last time a Canadiens' goalie played the entire season?
A. 1951–52—Gerry McNeil
B. 1961–62—Jacques Plante
C. 1969–70—Rogie Vachon
D. 1971–72—Ken Dryden

4.11 Why did coach Jacques Demers pull Patrick Roy during the overtime period in 1992–93's final regular season game?
A. He was protesting a call by referee Kerry Fraser.
B. He was resting Roy for the playoffs.
C. He was trying to finish higher in the standings.
D. He was testing backup goalie André Racicot for the playoffs.

4.12 Which goalie(s) captained the Canadiens?
A. George Hainsworth
B. Georges Vézina
C. Gerry McNeil
D. Bill Durnan

4.13 In how many games did Jacques Plante play without a mask after wearing it for the first time in 1959?
A. No games; Plante never played another "maskless" game.
B. Only one game
C. Two games, a back-to-back Boston series
D. 70 games, the entire 1961-62 season

4.14 What NHL first is shared by Richard Sevigny, Michel Larocque, Denis Herron and Rick Wamsley?
A. It was the first time four goalies all played regularly and were traded in the same season.
B. It was the first time four goalies each recorded a point in the same season for the same team.
C. It was the first time four goalies each recorded a shutout in the same season for the same team.
D. It was the first time four goalies won back-to-back games against their former teams in the same season.

4.15 In which Stanley Cup final series did Scotty Bowman bench Ken Dryden?
A. The 1973 Canadiens–Blackhawks finals
B. The 1976 Canadiens–Flyers finals
C. The 1978 Canadiens–Bruins finals
D. The 1979 Canadiens–Rangers finals

4.16 Which Canadiens' goaltender has the most points in regular season play?
A. Patrick Roy
B. Michel Larocque
C. Jacques Plante
D. Ken Dryden

JAKE THE SNAKE, ST. PATRICK AND OTHER GOALIE GREATS
Answers

4.1 A & D. Ken Dryden and Jacques Plante.
The best statistical argument that goalies peak during dynasty years (at least on the Canadiens) is the record for most season wins by Plante and Dryden, who hold down the top six spots—almost all in Cup-winning streaks. Their mark is five wins short of Bernie Parent's NHL record of 47 victories in 1973-74.

Player	Season	GP	W	L	T	GA	AVG.
CANADIENS TOP GOALIES/MOST SEASON-WINS							
1. J. Plante	1955–56	64	42	12	10	119	1.86
2. K. Dryden	1975–76	62	42	10	8	121	2.03
3. J. Plante	1961–62	70	42	14	14	166	2.37
4. K. Dryden	1976–77	56	41	6	8	117	2.14
5. J. Plante	1959–60	69	40	17	12	175	2.54
6. K. Dryden	1971–72	64	39	8	15	142	2.24
7. B. Durnan	1943–44	50	38	5	7	109	2.18

Current to 1993–94

4.2 C. The NHL's first-ever shutout.
In a game storied with heroes and legends, few players have been immortalized with greater distinction than Georges Vézina, the first of the Canadiens' greatest goaltenders. His name represents the highest order of excellence an NHL goalie can achieve, the Vézina Trophy. A man of quiet resolve, Vézina would have easily won the award named in his honour during his era of hockey. Always a Canadien, among his many achievements, three months into the NHL's first season, Vézina recorded the new league's first shutout, blanking the Toronto Arenas 9–0 on February 18, 1918.

4.3   A. A Los Angeles King.

Roy, himself surprised by the gesture, admitted the wink was unusual, especially during overtime in the Stanley Cup playoffs. Late in the extra period in game four with the Kings knocking, Roy stole one off a blast from Luc Robitaille. Sandstrom was there again in Roy's goalmouth, digging and sticking in vain for the lose puck. As Sandstrom glided half-cocked in the face-off circle before play resumed, he sneaked a weary look at Roy who telegraphed back an eyelash flick that impishly said: "Not tonight." The wink, inadvertently caught by an ice-level television camera, became one of the most celebrated TV shots of the 1993 playoffs.

4.4   D. More than five times.

The first time in NHL history siblings faced each other as opposing goalies was on March 20, 1971 when Ken, subbing for an injured Rogie Vachon, played against his elder brother Dave. Looking to make hockey history, Sabres coach Punch Imlach responded to the Canadiens switch by pulling Joe Daley and playing Dave opposite Ken, much to the thrill of Forum fans. After the 5-2 Canadiens win, the two Drydens skated to centre ice and, in an unusual gesture for regular season play, shook hands. Another NHL first was marked in the 1973 playoffs when the two brothers opposed each other twice in Stanley Cup play.

KEN VS. DAVE'S SIX EXCELLENT ADVENTURES			
	Shots Against		Score
Date	Ken	Dave	Habs–Sabres
1. 3/20/1971	33	31	5–2
2. 10/28/1972	31	31	3–3
3. 12/10/1972	28	28	2–4
4. 3/17/1973	34	41	3–3
5. 4/4/1973	32	36	2–1
6. 4/5/1973	23	35	7–3

4.5　B. Denis Herron.

In the 1970s when Lafleur recorded six consecutive 50-goal seasons, his favourite target was Herron, who, while playing with Pittsburgh and Kansas City, let in a hat trick of 50th Lafleur goals in 1975, 1976 and 1979. Mercifully, Herron's bad luck changed upon being traded to the Canadiens in 1979–80. But it was a brief respite from 50-goal scorers. Back in Pittsburgh a few years later, Herron fell victim on three more occasions to 50th goals by Michel Goulet, Tim Kerr and Wayne Gretzky.

4.6　A. Bill Durnan.

After Durnan blanked Detroit 1–0, Boston 4–0 and 1–0 and New York 3–0 in succession in 1948–49, it looked like Alex Connell's old 1928 record of six consecutive shutouts (461 minutes, 29 seconds) might be broken. But Durnan's hot streak ended in the next game at 5:36 of the second period when Gaye Stewart scored for Chicago. Montréal fans were disappointed, but because Connell's time totals happened before the centre red line was introduced, Durnan, today, is credited with the NHL's longest "modern-day" shutout sequence: 309 minutes, 21 seconds.

4.7　C. Charlie Hodge.

Hodge and Canadiens backup Gary Bauman are the only netminders in All-Star history to record a shutout, blanking the NHL's best 3–0 in 1967, the next-to-last year the All-Star format pitted the defending Cup champions against the rest of the league.

4.8　A. None.

In 1969 GM Sam Pollock paid the Bruins $25,000 for the rights to Dryden (who was on waivers after being originally drafted by Boston in 1964), a bit of deft planning that anchored the Canadiens into the next decade. After lacklustre performances by Rogie Vachon and Phil Myre, coach Al MacNeil called up Dryden on March 14, 1971 to play against the Penguins. The 5–1 victory salted MacNeil's opinion of the big rookie who allowed only nine goals in six games, all wins (including one against brother Dave). His 1.65 GAA signaled the beginning of the Ken Dryden era. And the end for Vachon, Myre and all the other backups who watched and waited without hope during Dryden's eight remarkable seasons.

4.9 D. George Hainsworth.

Much like the adoration bestowed on Patrick Roy, in the 1920s and '30s, Montréal fans championed the goaltending heroics of Hainsworth, who recorded 75 shutouts over seven full seasons. In his best year, 1928–29, the diminutive, "almost mechanical" Hainsworth zeroed the opposition an astonishing 22 times in the 44-game schedule to claim his third straight Vézina Trophy.

CANADIENS TOP SHUTOUT LEADERS

Player	Games	Seasons	SO
1. G. Hainsworth	321	1926–37	75
2. J. Plante	556	1952–63	58
3. K. Dryden	397	1970–79	46
4. B. Durnan	383	1943–50	34
5. G. McNeil	276	1947–57	28
6. P. Roy *	486	1984–	27

* *Active/current to 1993-94*

4.10 B. 1961–62—Jacques Plante.
Plante was the last Canadien goalie to play every season game, working all 70 matches in 1961–62. Prior to Plante, McNeil worked all 70 contests in 1951–52. Dryden managed 64 games in 1971–72 (78-game schedule) and Vachon, 64 matches in 1969–70 (76-game schedule).

4.11 C. He was trying to finish higher in the standings.
There aren't too many valid reasons for an NHL coach to pull a goalie in overtime and chance a loss instead of a one-point tie in regular season, except if it meant improving team point totals for a better playoff position. For Demers a tie wasn't going help the Canadiens finish ahead of Québec, a team two points up on Montréal but with one fewer win. With nothing to lose and playoff home ice advantage at stake, Roy was yanked for the extra attacker in overtime. But at the 4:12 mark, the gamble went bust. Washington's Mike Ridley pin-pointed a shot into the open net, bursting the Canadiens bubble and instantly becoming fodder for hockey trivia buffs.

4.12 A & D. George Hainsworth and Bill Durnan.
In NHL history only three goalies have ever been named team captain; the Canadiens have had two. Both Hainsworth (1932–33) and Durnan (1948, Jan.-Apr.) wore the "C" while tending goal. Although they backstopped in different decades, Hainsworth is indirectly connected to Durnan's captaincy. In 1933 Hainsworth was traded to Toronto for goalie Lorne Chabot who, two years later, was traded to the Montréal Maroons for Toe Blake. Blake captained the Canadiens from 1940 until January 11, 1948 when he suffered a career-ending injury. Coach Dick Irvin and the players picked the best man to captain his team and on January 15, Durnan

stepped into the crease wearing the "C." Who was the NHL's third goalie captain? Chicago's Charlie Gardiner in 1934.

4.13 B. Only one game.
Plante won seven Vézina Trophies, six Stanley Cups and one Hart Trophy in his 19 pro years, but he is best remembered for hockey's first goalie mask. After that momentous occasion on November 1, 1959, Plante's 11-game unbeaten streak served notice that masks neither impaired eyesight nor implied cowardice. Nevertheless, coach Toe Blake's misgivings forced a nervous, mask-less Plante between the pipes once more later that season. The 3–0 loss to Detroit on March 8, 1960 was the last time Plante barefaced the opposition, either from on-ice shooters or the skeptics who always asked, "Doesn't the mask prove you're scared?" Each time Plante responded, "If you jumped out of a plane without a parachute, would that make you brave?"

4.14 C. It was the first time four goalies each recorded a shutout in the same season for the same team.
During the dry years between Ken Dryden and Patrick Roy, the Canadiens tried out anyone with goalie pads in their search for a number one netminder. Larocque, the best in this gang of four, was fine as long as he backed up Dryden; Sevigny, Herron and Wamsley came and went in five disappointing years; but each recorded at least one shutout with the Canadiens in 1980–81. It was an NHL first and the only year three goalies won the Vézina, the absentee goalkeeper being Rick Wamsley, who played just five games.

4.15 D. The 1979 Canadiens–Rangers finals.
Dryden was technically benched twice in his playoff career, but the record shows only one period missed. On May 13, 1979 he sat out the third frame after falling

behind the Rangers 4-1 on 13 shots in game one of the Stanley Cup finals. Michel Larocque was handed game two, but an errant shot by Doug Risebrough during warm-up knocked him flat-out cold. Dryden stepped in and immediately dropped two goals on two shots after seven minutes of work. The New York bench was electric, but momentum shifted as the Rangers got caught sitting back on three quick Montréal scores. The Canadiens regrouped, backing Dryden, who won the next four straight for the Canadiens' fourth consecutive Cup.

4.16   A. Patrick Roy.

Although Plante became the NHL's first roving netminder (so nicknamed, Jake the Snake) and the first to headman the puck, his career points are low compared to other modern-day goalies like Roy, who benefits from a quicker transitional game and defensemen more skilled at carrying and moving the puck up ice.

		Regular	
Player	**Season**	**Season**	**Playoffs**
1. P. Roy *	1984–	27 A	4 A
2. K. Dryden	1971–79	19 A	5 A
3. M. Larocque	1973–80	12 A	2 A
4. J. Plante	1952–63	2 A	0
5. R. Vachon	1966–72	1 A	0
6. L. Worsley	1963–70	1 A	0

CANADIENS TOP GOALIE POINT-GETTERS

* *Active/current to 1993-94*

THE ALL-STAR GAME

Since 1930, 39 Canadiens have been selected to the NHL's first and second All-Star teams. The annual All-Star game has been played in several formats since its inception on February 14, 1934, when the NHL organized a benefit game for Toronto's Ace Bailey, the first Leaf ever to win the scoring championship. Bailey, who had suffered a career-ending head injury only months earlier, was there for the ceremonial faceoff.

Almost all of the Canadiens ever voted to the NHL's All-Star teams, listed below, appear in the puzzle, horizontally, vertically, diagonally or backwards. After you've circled all of the players, like Robinson and Harvey, the 26 leftover letters in the puzzle spell out in descending sequence: 1) the only missing Canadien All-Star team member, 2) a famous team nickname and 3) the secret word. (Be sure to circle the extra listed words, All, Star and Team in the puzzle.)

(Solution is on page 117)

Béliveau	Harris	Mahovlich	Provost
Blake	Harvey	Mantha	Reardon
Bouchard	Hodge	McNeil	Richard
Chelios	Johnson	Moore	Robinson
Cournoyer	Joliat	Morenz	Roy
Cude	Lach	Mosdell	Savard
Durnan	Lafleur	Naslund	Shutt
Engblom	Laperriere	Olmstead	Talbot
Geoffrion	Lapointe	Plante	Tremblay
Harmon			Worsley
All	Star	Team	

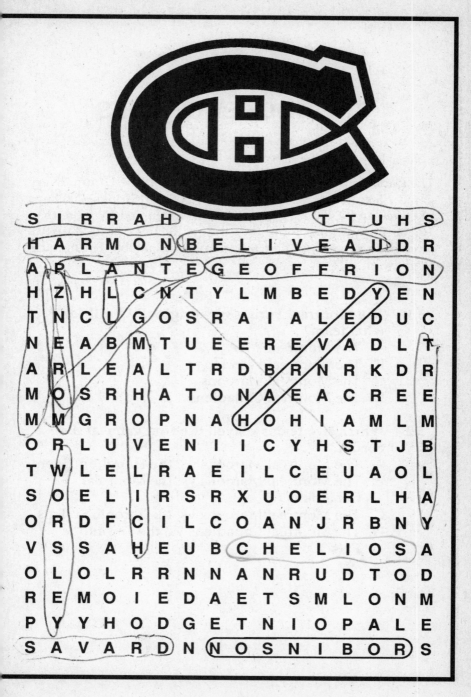

```
S I R R A H            T T U H S
H A R M O N B E L I V E A U D R
A P L A N T E G E O F F R I O N
H Z H L C N T Y L M B E D Y E N
T N C L G O S R A I A L E D U C
N E A B M T U E E R E V A D L T
A R L E A L T R D B R N R K D R
M O S R H A T O N A E A C R E E
M M G R O P N A H O H I A M L M
O R L U V E N I I C Y H S T J B
T W E L R A E I L C E U A O L L
S O E L I R S R X U O E R L H A
O R D F C I L C O A N J R B N Y
V S S A H E U B C H E L I O S A
O L O L R R N N A N R U D T O D
R E M O I E D A E T S M L O N M
P Y Y H O D G E T N I O P A L E
S A V A R D N N O S N I B O R S
```

5

THE HOCKEY SHRINES

The Canadiens have won 12 Stanley Cups at the Forum. Every game 7,500 hot dogs, 12,000 beers, 7,500 soft drinks, 700 cups of coffee and 2,400 ice cream bars are consumed by more than 16,000 Forum fans. Now that the really important statistics have been served up, here's some other palatable Forum facts to gnaw on.

(Answers are on page 54)

5.1 The Montréal Forum was originally built for what team?
A. The Montréal AAA
B. The Montréal Wanderers
C. The Montréal Maroons
D. The Montréal Canadiens

5.2 Which two teams played the first game at the Forum?
A. The Montréal Maroons vs. the Hamilton Tigers
B. The Montréal Maroons vs. the Montréal Canadiens
C. The Montréal Maroons vs. the Toronto St. Pats
D. The Montréal Canadiens vs. the Toronto St. Pats

5.3 **What was the original colour of all the seats at the Montréal Forum?**
   A. Blue
   B. Grey
   C. Brown
   D. Red

5.4 **What is so special about "Section 105/Row B/Seat 7" at the Forum?**
   A. It's Maurice Richard's box seat.
   B. It's Patrick Roy's lucky seat at practice.
   C. It's where all Canadian prime ministers and provincial premiers sit when attending Forum games.
   D. It's where Clarence Campbell was sitting before the Richard Riot.

5.5 **What happened on February 4, 1989?**
   A. Ronald Corey announces plans to move the Forum.
   B. Stéphane Richer becomes only the sixth Canadien to score 50 goals.
   C. Larry Robinson plays his final Forum game as a Canadien.
   D. Guy Lafleur returns to Forum ice.

5.6 **Where was the first Montréal Canadiens game played?**
   A. The Westmount Arena
   B. The Jubilee Rink
   C. The Mount Royal Arena
   D. The Montréal Arena

5.7 In what year did Roger Doucet first sing his new version of "O Canada" at the Forum?
A. 1974
B. 1976
C. 1978
D. 1980

5.8 It's been called "the greatest hockey game ever played." What were the shots on goal totals in the 3–3 tie between the Soviet Red Army and the Canadiens on New Year's Eve, December 31, 1975?
A. 13–13 shots apiece
B. 38–13 shots in favour of the Red Army
C. 38–13 shots in favour of the Canadiens
D. 38–38 shots apiece

5.9 During the Depression what sport, besides hockey, kept the Forum in business?
A. Lacrosse
B. Boxing
C. Roller Skating
D. Wrestling

5.10 What Montréal rink established the standard 200-foot by 85-foot dimensions for professional hockey in North America?
A. The Victoria Skating Rink
B. The Montréal Forum
C. The Jubilee Rink
D. The Mount Royal Arena

5.11 What is the rink floor made of in the Forum?
A. Limestone
B. Sand
C. Hardwood maple
D. Concrete

5.12 Who advertised on the old Forum score clock in the 1940s and 50s?
A. Seagram's
B. Molson Breweries
C. MacDonald Tobacco
D. Harold Cummings Automobile dealership

5.13 Which statement is incorrect?
A. The Montréal Forum is the oldest arena in the NHL.
B. The Forum was originally built at a cost of $1,500,000.
C. Frank Selke posted "To you from failing hands we throw the torch; be yours to hold it high," in the Canadiens' dressing room.
D. The Forum was last renovated in 1968.

5.14 What was the price of a seat (in the 1940s) in the old Millionaires Section at the Forum?
A. Less than one dollar
B. Two dollars
C. Five dollars
D. Ten dollars

5.15 In what year was the first Montréal Canadiens game televised at the Forum?
A. 1950
B. 1951
C. 1952
D. 1953

5.16 Which team won the first Stanley Cup awarded in Forum history?
A. The Montréal Canadiens in 1923–24
B. The Montréal Maroons in 1925–26
C. The New York Rangers in 1927–28
D. The Montréal Canadiens in 1929–30

5.17 In what year did the Canadiens begin wearing their white uniforms when they played at home?
A. 1948
B. 1958
C. 1968
D. 1978

5.18 How far back does the Forum's waiting list go for season ticket requests?
A. 1979
B. 1981
C. 1983
D. 1985

THE HOCKEY SHRINES
Answers

5.1 **C. The Montréal Maroons.**
The Forum was built in 1924 for the Canadiens' crosstown rivals and the NHL's newest team, the Maroons. Run by businessman Jimmy Strachan, the Maroons profited wildly from the box-office success of their "S" line of Nels Stewart, Babe Siebert and Hooley Smith, especially so whenever they played against the

Canadiens' great line of Morenz, Joliat and Black Cat Gagnon. The two Montréal teams began sharing the Forum in 1926 when the Canadiens officially made it their home rink. The Maroons folded in 1938.

5.2   D. The Montréal Canadiens vs. the Toronto St. Pats.

Much to their displeasure, the Maroons debut, scheduled for the Forum's inaugural game on December 3, 1924, was upstaged by the Canadiens, who moved their season opener (November 29th) to Atwater and St. Catherine because of poor ice conditions at their own rink, the Mount Royal Arena. Billy Boucher, the Canadiens only No. 13 ever, scored the Forum's very first goal (and hat trick) in a 7–1 win over the Toronto St. Pats. That goal began hockey's most enduring partnership, the Canadiens and the NHL's longest surviving arena, the Forum.

5.3   C. Brown.

Before Frank Selke dressed up the Forum with coloured red, blue and grey seating sections, everything, except the advertising billboards, was varnished or painted in brown. There were no individual box seats; fans sat on ugly brown benches or loose chairs at rinkside, each numbered by small white digits. The old Forum before 1948 lacked character, a dark and colourless venue.

5.4   B. It's Patrick Roy's lucky seat at practice.

At each practice during the 1992–93 playoff campaign, Roy sat in the same seat and row in Section 105 to analyze his opponents' shooting techniques. The ritual began after the first win against Québec and never altered, not even by a seat. "It's going to help me during a game to know if a player lowers his shoulder when he shoots high, or does something else," says Roy. Any good luck from it didn't hurt either.

5.5   D. Guy Lafleur returns to Forum ice.
Four years after he played his last Canadiens game at
the Forum, Lafleur returned as a New York Ranger and
gave Canadiens fans a night to remember. He drew an
assist on Dave Shaw's goal, then scored on a rebound
and, finally, with 17,231 fans poised for more déja-vu,
the 37-year-old Hall-of-Famer made two beautiful
deeks on Petr Svoboda and Rick Green, going in alone
to score his second goal on Patrick Roy. Two goals and
an assist on February 4, 1989. The Canadiens won the
game, but the night belonged to Lafleur.

5.6   B. The Jubilee Rink.
Before the Forum became their home rink, the
Canadiens' first games were played at the Jubilee Rink,
a small 2,700-seat arena at Moreau and St. Catherine in
Montréal. In their inaugural season, 1909–10, there
were already four other pro hockey teams in Montréal,
all sharing and competing for the city's few arenas.
Cramped, dank and smoke-filled, Jubilee Rink was the
Canadiens' first home, where, on January 5, 1910, they
won their first game, defeating Cobalt, Ontario, 7–6 in
overtime.

5.7   C. 1978.
He was called the "the golden voice with the silver
hair," and for 10 years Doucet never missed singing "O
Canada" at Canadiens' home games. In May 1978, with
Prime Minister Trudeau in attendance, Doucet per-
formed Canada's national anthem, changing the lyrics
"We stand on guard for thee" to "for rights and liberty."
It was probably the first time any singer formally
altered "O Canada" at a public event.

5.8   C. 38-13 shots in favour of the Canadiens.
At least two reputations were made on New Year's Eve
1975. Dryden, never at his best against the Soviets,
allowed three goals on 13 shots; while Vladislav Tretiak

fended off wave upon wave of the Canadiens' finest marksmen, stopping 35 shots on his way into the Hockey Hall of Fame. The Soviets rarely played against a team with such all-round defensive skills as the Canadiens. In the first two periods their fearsome attack netted just seven shots on goal. Tretiak stood on his head and stopped almost everything, including 16 shots in the third period and three quick, point-blank howitzers while his team was shorthanded.

5.9   D. Wrestling.

With the Forum mortgaged to the limit, hockey alone couldn't pay the bills in the 1930s. So in the summer and fall, Tommy Gorman, manager of the Canadian Arena Company, turned a profit on headlocks, half-nelsons and pile drivers: the show-stopping stuff of professional wrestling.

5.10   A. The Victoria Skating Rink.

Long before the first organized hockey team was formed at McGill University in 1879 and, certainly, when garrison troops in Halifax and Kingston were developing ice hockey from rugby, Montréal's Victoria Rink was hosting elaborate skating parties for as many as 1500 "gaily dressed" guests under its cathedral-like arched roof and viewing galleries. With its 200-foot by 85-foot ice surface it was considered the largest and best rink in either Europe or North America. As hockey evolved from rudimentary conditions outdoors to indoor facilities, rules developed and "the silvery floor of ice" at Victoria Rink quickly attracted enthusiasts for competitive play. Although many towns disagree, Victoria Rink hosted the first "public exhibition" of organized hockey on March 3, 1875. A McGill student, J.G.A. Creighton, who played in that game and later became a prominent lawyer, is credited with originating the McGill Rules, the foundation upon which today's game evolved, including the standard 200-foot by 85-foot dimensions.

5.11 B. Sand.

The only NHL arena without a concrete slab floor below rink level is the Montréal Forum. It still uses a 3-inch thick sand base to carry the 1½-inch thick, 200-foot by 85-foot ice surface. The sand is imbedded with 11 miles of 1¼-inch refrigeration pipes or "brines" which cool the ice (demineralized water) at 28°F. During a game the brine, ice and house temperatures are monitored for heat gain. Below the sand is a 6 mm plastic vapour barrier on top of two inches of styrofoam insulation which covers the subsoil. The new Montréal Forum is designed with a concrete floor.

5.12 C. MacDonald Tobacco.

For many a hockey oldtimer the image is burned in memory. At the Forum's south end, advertised below the penalty minute hands on the old score clock, is the familiar twin Export "A" packs with the cameo of a Scottish highland lass, a smouldering cigarette and the MacDonald Tobacco emblem.

5.13 C. Frank Selke posted "To you from failing hands we throw the torch; be yours to hold it high," in the Canadiens dressing room.

In fact, it was coach Dick Irvin who borrowed poet John McCrae's famous words from "In Flanders Fields" and posted them above the player's benches in the Canadiens dressing room. Today, 40 years later, the bilingual message is still there. Inscribed on a photomontage of Canadiens greats, it represents the building blocks of tradition for sport's winningest franchise.

5.14 A. Less than one dollar.

In the 1940s the best hockey action in the NHL could be had for 50 cents, the price of standing room or a seat on a bench in the Millionaire's Section (4,500 capacity) at the Forum's north end. But Frank Selke's celebrated 1948–49 reno-job enlarged the Forum, raised seating capacity from 9600 to 12,500 and eliminated the famous Millionaire's Section and 50 cent ticket prices.

5.15 C. 1952.

For those few Québec families with televisions, the grainy black-and-white images that flickered into their homes on October 9, 1952 were nothing short of miraculous. Live from the Forum, they saw their beloved Canadiens play the Blackhawks in a game called by legendary play-by-play announcer René Lecavalier. The Canadiens English voice, Danny Gallivan, started his 32-year career that night. The broadcast was marred only by the final score: Hawks 3–Habs 2. Today 90% of Canadiens games are televised.

5.16 B. The Montréal Maroons in 1925–26.

Besides the 24 Stanley Cup banners hanging from the Forum rafters, it's long been considered (though never too seriously) that a few are missing: two orange-and-maroon "Ms" for Montréal's other Cup-winning team, the forgotten 1926 and 1935 Maroons. After all, the Forum was the Maroons' home rink first in 1924, and they won the Forum's first Cup in 1925–26. In fact, the 1929–30 Canadiens aren't even the second team to parade the Stanley Cup on Forum ice. Two years before, the 1927–28 Rangers won the championship at Atwater and St. Catherine by defeating the Maroons in the best-of-five final series.

5.17 C. 1968.

The white uniform, first worn in 1945 for road games, became the team's home jersey in 1968. The original white sweater's blue band across the chest was eliminated during the 1950s, replaced by red shoulder inserts and narrow red and blue bands across the bottom.

5.18 A. 1979.

The oldest request for season tickets on the Forum's waiting list of 3,100 names dates back to June 1979. The request stipulates "a pair of reds," which is in the best section, 17 rows deep from ice level. The long wait could be over. The new Forum accommodates 21,000 fans.

THE CAPTAINS

In Canadiens' history, at least 14 players have captained the team. Reading across, down or diagonally, find their names by connecting lines between letters, like C-L-E-G-H-O-R-N, and start with the letters in heavy type.

(Solution is on page 118)

6

SUPERSTAR SNIPERS

There was no one more dangerous from the blueline in then Maurice Richard. His coal-black eyes lit up like pinball lights when he bore down on a goalie. His speed accelerated the play around an opponent's net, creating a whirlwind of action just before his shot, forehand or backhand, would deliver a pass or blow a goalie off his feet.

All superstars can turn a game around, or up a notch, by scoring the comeback goal or making the big pin-point pass. From Howie Morenz to Guy Lafleur, the Canadiens have been blessed with stars of great calibre. Like The Rocket, they have all played with that fierce intensity belonging only to champions.

(Answers are on page 65)

6.1 Whose jersey was retired first by the Canadiens?
A. Aurèle Joliat's No. 4
B. Howie Morenz's No. 7
C. Maurice Richard's No. 9
D. Elmer Lach's No. 16

6.2 Who was the youngest Canadien to score a 50-goal season?
A. Bernie Geoffrion
B. Guy Lafleur
C. Steve Shutt
D. Stéphane Richer

6.3 **Which Canadiens' line holds the record for most points-per-game average?**
A. Joliat-Morenz-Larochelle, 1929–30
B. Blake-Lach-Richard, 1944–45
C. Olmstead-Béliveau-Geoffrion, 1955–56
D. Shutt-Lemaire-Lafleur, 1976–77

6.4 **Which Canadien rookie led all team members in goal scoring in his first season?**
A. Jean Béliveau
B. Maurice Richard
C. Dickie Moore
D. Bernie Geoffrion

6.5 **Guy Lafleur was the first Canadien to record a 100-point season. Who was the second?**
A. Steve Shutt
B. Henri Richard
C. Pete Mahovlich
D. Jacques Lemaire

6.6 **Besides Guy Lafleur, Steve Shutt and Pete Mahovlich, who is the only other (and most recent) Canadien with a 100-point season?**
A. Mats Naslund
B. Bobby Smith
C. Stéphane Richer
D. Vincent Damphousse

6.7 **Which NHL goalie was most often scored against by Maurice Richard during his 50-goals-in-50-games drive?**
A. Detroit's Harry Lumley
B. Chicago's Mike Karakas
C. Toronto's Frank McCool
D. New York's Ken McAuley

6.8 In what season did Guy Lafleur break Maurice Richard's 544-goal mark?
A. 1983–84, as a Canadien
B. 1988–89, as a Ranger
C. 1989–90, as a Nordique
D. 1990–91, as a Nordique

6.9 What do Gordie Howe and Jean Béliveau share in common?
A. Both scored All-Star game-winning goals.
B. Both wore identical jersey numbers at one point in their NHL careers.
C. Each led the league in penalty minutes the same year they finished first in NHL scoring.
D. Each finished runner-up to the other in the NHL scoring race.

6.10 Who was the last Canadiens' player to score five goals in one game?
A. Yvan Cournoyer
B. Henri Richard
C. Russ Courtnall
D. Kirk Muller

6.11 Besides Guy Lafleur, who was the only other Canadien ever to win the NHL's scoring title in two consecutive years?
A. Newsy Lalonde
B. Bernie Geoffrion
C. Dickie Moore
D. Jean Béliveau

6.12 Which Canadiens' team placed the most players on the NHL's First All-Star team?
A. The 1944–45 Canadiens
B. The 1955–56 Canadiens
C. The 1958–59 Canadiens
D. The 1976–77 Canadiens

6.13 What broke up The Punch Line?
A. Maurice Richard's first NHL suspension in 1947
B. Toe Blake's career-ending injury
C. Coach Dick Irvin's new line combinations
D. Elmer Lach's career-ending injury

6.14 Which Canadien scored the fastest hat trick in team history?
A. Dickie Moore
B. Vincent Damphousse
C. Black Cat Gagnon
D. Jean Béliveau

6.15 Which Canadiens' superstar was once named all three stars in a game.
A. Aurèle Joliat
B. Guy Lafleur
C. Joe Malone
D. Maurice Richard

SUPERSTAR SNIPERS
Answers

6.1 B. Howie Morenz's No. 7.
In almost 85 years the Canadiens have retired only six numbers, worn by eight players. A surprise, considering all the Hall of Famers and Cup champions that have graced the famous bleu-blanc-rouge CH over the years. That privilege first went to No. 7, the Canadiens' first superstar, Howie Morenz. For 14 NHL seasons Morenz illuminated the game with his speed and flash, capturing the imagination of the hockey world, and then suddenly sending it into mourning in 1937. Months earlier, Morenz had snapped his leg just above

the ankle after crashing into the boards with Chicago's Earl Seibert. Despite his upbeat mood at Montréal's St. Luc Hospital, Morenz privately confessed to linemate Aurèle Joliat that he might never play hockey again. Officially, Morenz died of a coronary embolism, but Joliat often said, "I think Howie died of a broken heart." The Golden Age of Sports produced many superb athletes, and like Babe Ruth, Jack Dempsey and Red Grange in their respective sports, Morenz dominated his game and ignited the mythical torch to hand down to the next generation of Flying Frenchmen. On November 2, 1937 the Canadiens retired Howie Morenz's No. 7. It was only the second jersey so honoured in professional hockey.

6.2   D. Stéphane Richer.
Richer was only 21 years, 10 months old when he recorded his first 50-goal season in 1988. Not young enough to beat Wayne Gretzky (19 years, 2 months), Jimmy Carson (19 years, 7 months) or Pierre Larouche (20 years, 5 months) overall in the NHL but easily the Canadiens' youngest, ahead of Lafleur (23 years, 6 months), Richard (23 years, 7 months) and Shutt (24 years, 8 months).

6.3   B. Blake-Lach-Richard, 1944–45.
The Punch Line, Elmer Lach centering Toe Blake and Maurice Richard, overwhelmed the NHL in 1944–45, averaging an unbelievable 4.4 points per game and finishing 1–2–3 in league scoring (Lach–80, Richard–73, Blake–67). No threesome in league history has ever topped that mark—although it has been matched by the Kings' Triple Crown Line (Dave Taylor, Marcel Dionne and Charlie Simmer) and the Islanders' Grande Trio (Clark Gillies, Bryan Trottier and Mike Bossy).

THE CANADIENS TOP SCORING LINES
(from four hockey eras)

Line	Year	Games	Points	Avg.
Blake-Lach-Richard	1944–45	50	220	**4.40**
Shutt-Lemaire-Lafleur	1976–77	80	316	**3.95**
Olmstead-Béliveau-Geoffrion	1955–56	70	220	**3.14**
Joliat-Morenz-Larochelle	1929–30	44	106	**2.41**

6.4   D. Bernie Geoffrion.

Geoffrion is one of very few NHLers ever to score more goals in his rookie season than any other member on his first full-year team. Boom-Boom's bullet shot and lightning-quick stickhandling earned him 30 goals (and 54 points) in 67 games in 1951–52, strong enough to finish first in team goals and second in team scoring behind veteran Elmer Lach (15–50–65). In that season, fellow rookie Dickie Moore established his presence on the Canadiens, scoring 18 goals in just 33 games.

6.5   C. Pete Mahovlich.

Centering Lafleur and Shutt, Mahovlich played his best NHL season in 1974–75 when he scored 117 points (35 goals–82 assists). Little M scored his 100th point on March 9, 1975, just two days—one game—after Lafleur became the Canadiens' very first 100-point man on March 7. It was Lafleur's 56th game of 1974–75 and Mahovlich's 67th.

6.6   A. Mats Naslund.

The Canadiens' first Swede in club history is the only other Canadien to earn 100 points in a season. Naslund's best record (43–67–110) came during the Canadiens' Stanley Cup-winning season in 1985–86. Lafleur recorded six 100-point seasons (1975–80), Mahovlich two (1975/76) and Naslund and Shutt (1976–77), one each.

6.7   A. Detroit's Harry Lumley.

Lumley's entry into the NHL was a baptism by fire. In his first game against the Canadiens on December 28, 1944, the Detroit rookie gave up five goals and three assists to Richard in the 9–1 shredding. Although Detroit finished second overall (to first place Montréal) in front of Lumley, the Red Wings only managed one victory in ten starts against the Habs. Richard, on track to score the NHL's first 50-in-50, had Lumley's number. It was 14 goals against; one record the other netminders cared not to challenge.

RICHARD'S 50-in-50 VICTIMS		
Player	Team	GA
1. Harry Lumley	Detroit	14
2. Mike Karakas	Chicago	8
3. Frank McCool	Toronto	8
4. Ken McAuley	New York	7
5. Harvey Bennett	Boston	6
6. Paul Bibeault	Boston	5
7. Connie Dion	Detroit	2

6.8   C. 1989–90, as a Nordique.

Despite producing a team-leading 1246 points on 518 goals and 728 assists, Lafleur always regretted not breaking Richard's 544-goal mark while with the Canadiens. Shy by only 26 goals, Lafleur began his comeback four years later with an 18-goal season in New York before moving on to Québec where, on January 3, 1990, he targeted his 545th NHL goal. It wouldn't effect Richard's record in the Canadiens stat books, but Lafleur's long-time objective had been partially realized. He kept the puck and in 1991 retired with 560 goals.

6.9 B. Both wore identical jersey numbers at one point in their NHL careers.

Despite the close association with their respective No. 9 and No. 4, neither Howe nor Béliveau started their careers with those numbers. In fact, each wore sweater No. 17 when they entered the league. In Howe's case, Detroit's jersey No. 9 only became available after his rookie season when Roy Conacher was dealt to Chicago. Béliveau, who wore No. 4 with the Québec Aces, was handed the Canadiens No. 17 for his two-game tryout in 1950–51. That season, three rookies (Claude Robert, Ernie Roche and Hugh Currie) shared the Habs' No. 4.

6.10 A. Yvan Cournoyer.

When Cournoyer scored five times on Chicago's Mike Veisor February 15, 1975, he became the ninth Hab in team history to record a five-goal game. In the 12-3 romp over the Hawks, coach Scotty Bowman juggled Cournoyer and several lines, combining him most often with Jacques Lemaire and Murray Wilson. The Roadrunner added two assists to the five goals, one point away from the team record for most points (8) in a game.

6.11 C. Dickie Moore.

Since 1918, eight Canadiens have won the league's scoring race 16 times, Lafleur the only triple consecutive champion and Moore the only other double winner to record back-to-back titles, in 1957–58 (36–48–84) and 1958–59 (41–55–96). Moore's puckhandling and skating skills (his fists and elbows, too) landed him on the Canadiens' best lines of the 1950s, playing alongside the Richard brothers or with Jean Béliveau and Bernie Geoffrion. He played 12 years and won six Cups.

6.12   A. The 1944–45 Canadiens.

In 60 years of all-star games, only the Canadiens and Chicago have ever placed five players on the NHL's First All-Star team in one year. In 1944–45, a Cup-less season for the Canadiens, they snagged five of six first all-star positions and best coach.

THE 1944-45 FIRST ALL-STAR TEAM

Player	Team	Position
Bill Durnan	Montréal	Goalie
Émile Bouchard	Montréal	Defense
Frank Hollett	Detroit	Defense
Elmer Lach	Montréal	Centre
Maurice Richard	Montréal	Right W
Toe Blake	Montréal	Left W
Dick Irvin	Montréal	Coach

6.13   B. Toe Blake's career-ending injury.

The Punch Line played together four seasons, each year a first overall finish, plus two Stanley Cups. But on January 11, 1948, Blake suffered a double fracture of the ankle after falling into the boards from a heavy check by New York defenseman Bill Juzda. He never played again, and The Punch Line was history. Oddly enough, his linemates each sustained broken legs, Richard earlier in his career and Lach in his final season.

6.14   D. Jean Béliveau.

On November 5, 1955 Béliveau put on an astonishing performance at the Forum when he scored all four Canadiens goals (in a 4–2 Bruins defeat), including three within 44 seconds on Boston's Terry Sawchuk. Béliveau's hat trick happened at :42, 1:08 and 1:26 of the second period while the Canadiens were holding a 6–4 man advantage. Although Bill Mosienko notched the

NHL's fastest hat trick in 21 seconds even-strength, Béliveau's three quick man-advantage markers proved the turning point for many hockey managers who petitioned the league to adopt a rule whereby penalized teams revert to normal strength when a goal is scored by the opposing team. Shortly after, Rule 27(c) was enacted and remains in effect today.

6.15 D. Maurice Richard.

On March 23, 1944, the night The Rocket scored five goals in a 5–1 playoff win over the Maple Leafs, there was little doubt who ruled the ice. After the game the three stars were announced as "Richard, Richard and Richard."

GAME 6

THE WONDER YEARS

Through the years, Canadiens have achieved many hockey firsts and witnessed many lasts, have broken umpteen records and celebrated some remarkable events, both individually and as a team.

In this game, match the events below with their dates.

(Solution is on page 118)

1920	1950	1962	1982
1923	1955	1968	1983
1936	1957	1973	1986
1945	1959	1977	1990
1947	1961	1979	1993

1. _____ Éric Desjardins scores the team's 15,000th NHL goal.
2. _____ Jean Béliveau is named Canadiens' captain.
3. _____ The year of the Richard Riot.
4. _____ Howie Morenz scores his first NHL goal.
5. _____ Mats Naslund becomes the first European to play regularly for the Canadiens.
6. _____ Toe Blake coaches his last Canadiens game.
7. _____ Maurice Richard becomes the first NHLer to record 500 regular season goals.

8. _____ Bernie Geoffrion coaches just 30 games for the Canadiens before retiring.

9. _____ Jacques Plante is named league MVP. He is the last goalie to win the Hart Trophy.

10. _____ Larry Robinson appears in his first Canadiens game.

11. _____ The longest game in NHL history—176 minutes and 36 seconds—is played at the Forum between Detroit and the Maroons.

12. _____ The Canadiens win the Stanley Cup, their 12th on Forum ice.

13. _____ Jean Béliveau and Bernie Geoffrion play in the Canadiens uniform for the first time.

14. _____ The Canadiens trounce the Québec Bulldogs 16-3, an NHL record for most goals by one team in one game.

15. _____ Doug Harvey makes his debut at the Forum.

16. _____ The Canadiens register an NHL record 132-point season.

17. _____ Jacques Plante wears the NHL's first goalie mask.

18. _____ Guy Lafleur and Steve Shutt reach milestones in the same game, recording their 500th and 400th career goals respectively.

19. _____ The Canadiens become the first NHL team to record 5,000 team points.

20. _____ Maurice Richard scores his 50th goal in 50 games.

7

NO HOLDS BARRED

Being a mean son of a bitch didn't start with John Ferguson. Long before he arrived in 1963 to play team enforcer, the Canadiens were winning championships not by finesse and speed alone, but with heavy hitting and gritty play along the boards, in the corners and at the goalmouth. The Canadiens had to muscle their way through the league year after year to be consistent winners.

(Answers are on page 78)

7.1 **How many times was Maurice Richard suspended or fined during his career?**
A. Only once
B. Five times
C. Seven times
D. More than seven times

7.2 **Which Canadien has the most career penalty minutes?**
A. John Ferguson
B. Mario Tremblay
C. Chris Nilan
D. Émile "Butch" Bouchard

7.3 **What NHL first does John Ferguson hold?**
A. The first triple minor in NHL history
B. The quickest game misconduct in a rookie career
C. The quickest suspension in a rookie season
D. The first game misconduct for leaving the penalty box.

7.4 **What else did Jean Béliveau accomplish the season he recorded his highest career penalty minute totals?**
A. He was suspended the only time in his career.
B. He won his only Art Ross Trophy as NHL scoring leader.
C. He wore his famous No. 4 jersey for the first time.
D. He led all NHLers in penalty minutes.

7.5 **Which Canadien had his nose broken in a big fight with Bruin Stan Jonathan during the 1978 Cup finals?**
A. Bill Nyrop
B. Pierre Bouchard
C. Yvon Lambert
D. Réjean Houle

7.6 **Who was the first patient Canadiens' physician Dr. Doug Kinnear treated for an on-ice injury?**
A. Charlie Hodge
B. Referee Art Skov
C. Claude Provost
D. Canadiens' trainer Larry Aubut

7.7 **Which goalie recorded the most penalty minutes in Canadiens' history?**
A. Patrick Roy
B. Jacques Plante
C. Pierre Sevigny
D. Brian Hayward

7.8 How much were the Canadiens and Flyers fined in total for their pre-game brawl in the 1987 playoffs?
A. $4,000
B. $8,000
C. $12,000
D. $24,000

7.9 Which incident in the 1950s provoked Maurice Richard into publicly calling NHL president Clarence Campbell "a dictator?"
A. A suspension to teammate Bernie Geoffrion
B. An NHL rule change on fighting
C. His suspension before the Richard Riot
D. A referee switch during the playoffs

7.10 Who was fined for slugging a referee during the 1961 playoffs?
A. Doug Harvey
B. Claude Provost
C. Albert Langlois
D. Toe Blake

7.11 Which modern-day Canadiens' skater has the fewest penalty minutes in the most games (minimum 500)?
A. Floyd Curry
B. Jacques Lemaire
C. Donnie Marshall
D. Yvan Cournoyer

7.12 In John Ferguson's first NHL fight, he took on the Bruins' Ted Green, pulling the sweater over his head before trashing him. Afterwards, Green was interviewed on television and asked what it was like when Fergie had the sweater over his head. What did Green say?
A. "It was dark."
B. "Who turned out the . . . ?"
C. "John who?"
D. "Fight. What fight?"

7.13 What were Forum fans yelling during the Canadiens–Red Wings game the night of the Richard Riot?
A. "Go Habs Go."
B. "Les Canadiens Sont Là." (Canadiens all the way!)
C. "On veut Richard—à bas Campbell." (We want Richard—Down with Campbell)
D. "Campbell est un chien sal." (Campbell is a dirty dog.)

7.14 Who is the only Canadiens' player ever kissed by broadcaster Don Cherry?
A. Chris Nilan
B. Todd Ewen
C. Doug Jarvis
D. Chris Chelios

NO HOLDS BARRED
Answers

7.1   D. More than seven times.

The Richard Riot is remembered for its widespread violence and its primary cause, the 1955 playoff suspension to the Rocket; but it was also the apex of a series of game misconducts, suspensions and fines levelled at Richard for past altercations with opponents and officials alike. The Rocket was the NHL's biggest single attraction, and he paid for that privilege every night, fighting his way through the league to play at the top of his game. Hockey archivist/writer Charles Coleman describes one Richard fight in *The Trail of the Stanley Cup*: "In the final period, Richard was tripped and rose with a cut between the eyes. No penalty was given and Richard argued with referee McLean and, when he did not desist, was given a misconduct penalty. The Rocket became incensed when he entered the box and found (Detroit's) Leo Reise there to welcome him with some derisive remarks. Richard replied with a punch and, when the linesman rushed to intervene, the infuriated Canadien player (Richard) poked at him with the result that the penalty was raised to a game misconduct." The story doesn't end there, the next morning in a hotel lobby, it's alleged Richard grabbed McLean by the tie, for which president Campbell later fined the Rocket $500 for "conduct prejudicial to the welfare of hockey." Not the kind of action befitting the game's superstar, but in those days there were no Marty McSorleys to look after your Wayne Gretzkys; you fought your own battles, more or less. And the temperamental Richard had plenty: two suspensions, three game misconducts and eight separate fines. In fact, Richard is the second most penalized Canadien in team history with 1285 PIM.

7.2 C. Chris Nilan.

This might be one of our easiest answers. Nilan leads all Canadien combatants with 2248 PIM, almost double second-place Richard (1285 PIM), Ferguson (1214 PIM), Tremblay (1043 PIM) or Bouchard (863 PIM). Nilan was also the first Canadien to eclipse 200 penalty minutes in a season (1980–81).

7.3 A. The first triple minor in NHL history.

It's a wonder it hadn't happened sooner to Ferguson, who was assessed the first triple minor in NHL history for high-sticking, charging and slashing Gary Bergman in a 2–2 Canadiens' tie against Detroit at the Forum on December 7, 1967, four seasons into his career busting chops as Habs' designated enforcer.

7.4 B. He won his only Art Ross Trophy as NHL scoring leader.

It's remembered as the year Béliveau "got tough." After enduring two seasons of punishment without retaliating, Béliveau went into 1955–56 with a new attitude: repay every challenger and meet with equal physical force; no cheek-turning. For that, Béliveau amassed 143 penalty minutes, a personal record and good enough for third highest in the league. But his physical presence also helped establish his superstar status, winning the scoring race (47–41–88), the Hart Trophy as league MVP, the Stanley Cup and First All-Star team centre position. After his rookie "testing period" Béliveau rarely had to prove himself physically again.

7.5 B. Pierre Bouchard.

To twist an old hockey adage, "If you can't beat 'em on the ice, beat 'em in the alley," is what the Bruins had in mind in the fourth and get-even game of the 1978 Cup finals. Tied 1-1 in the game but down 2–1 in the series, Boston pulled the Canadiens off their finesse game into a round of fights that sent Gilles Lupien and John Wensink into the box for gross misconduct and fighting penalties. Then, the best match-up (and "a close one" according to Don Cherry) pitted Jonathan against Bouchard who got walloped on the beak late in the fight. It blew off a little steam and created the intended Bruin turnaround: Boston won 4–3 in overtime. And Bouchard lost; one broken nose and see-ya next year.

7.6 C. Claude Provost.

As Canadiens physician for more than 30 years, Dr. Doug Kinnear has witnessed every team ailment and injury, from Lou Fontinato's 1963 career-ending crash into the boards to Patrick Roy's appendicitis bout in 1994. His first glimpse into hockey machismo came in his first game when Claude Provost needed stitch work to close a deep two-inch laceration on his forehead. Kinnear asked for local anaesthetic before stitching the gash, but therapist Bill Head shook off the request, implying that cuts don't require freezing. Kinnear breathed deeply and with needle and suture sewed up the gaping wound. Provost was back on the ice for his next shift, to Kinnear's amazement.

7.7 A. Patrick Roy.

Roy leads all Canadiens netminders in penalties with 84 minutes; his highest season total, 30 penalty minutes, occured in 1993–94. Next highest are: Plante (72 PIM), Sevigny (64 PIM) and Hayward (40 PIM).

7.8 D. $24,000.

Officials handed out $24,000 in fines to the Flyers and Canadiens involved in an pre-game brawl after Claude Lemieux tried to take his customary warm-up shot into Philadelphia's net. The last players off the ice, Chico Resch and Ed Hospodar, mugged Lemieux and Shayne

Corson; players, half-undressed, piled out of the dressing rooms to rescue their teammates. The mêlée lasted 11 minutes before order was restored.

7.9   A. A suspension to teammate Bernie Geoffrion.
Richard was so infuriated by Campbell's seven-game suspension to Geoffrion (for a stick-swinging incident with Rangers' Ron Murphy), he called the league president "a dictator" and threatened to retire unless his linemate was reinstated. Worse, Richard made the comments in his ghost written newspaper column in Montréal's *Samedi Dimanche*. The furore died down only after Richard apologized and quit his weekly column.

7.10   D. Toe Blake.
In the 1961 semi-finals a lot was at stake between Chicago and Montréal. The Canadiens sought a record sixth straight Cup; the Hawks, a mixture of veterans and hungry new bloods, were looking for Chicago's first championship since 1938. Game three proved the series' turning point. It took triple overtime before the Hawks' Murray Balfour popped the power play winner behind Jacques Plante. Blake was so incensed at the officiating of referee Dalton McArthur, who had disallowed an earlier overtime Habs goal, that he charged onto the ice after the game and drilled the official in front of a jammed Chicago Stadium. Blake's fine? $2,000.

7.11   C. Donnie Marshall.
Marshall is the Canadiens all-time choirboy. Outright. And irrefutable considering in 10 seasons and 585 games, he amassed a wimpishly low 81 penalty minutes, far less than Curry (147 PIM in 601 games), Lemaire (217 PIM/853 games) or Cournoyer (255 PIM/968 games), the next least penalized 500-game Canadiens.

7.12 A. "It was dark."

Said half in humour, half in pain, when the lights went out on Ted Green, it signalled a new hockey era: the NHL's first policeman has arrived.

7.13 C. "On veut Richard—à bas Campbell." (We want Richard—Down with Campbell.)

Despite the verbal abuse and death threats to Clarence Campbell in the wake of his 1955 suspension to Maurice Richard, the league president still attended the next Canadiens match at the Forum. It was just the spark needed by angry fans who showered Campbell with debris and taunted "On veut Richard—à bas Campbell." But the worst was yet to come. A tear gas canister exploded near Campbell and the Forum was evacuated. Downtown stores were trashed, several police cars damaged and dozens arrested in the subsequent riot. Glass littered St. Catherine for 20 city blocks between Atwater and University.

7.14 A. Chris Nilan.

It couldn't happen to a nicer Bostonian; or on a better occasion. During the second intermission and the Canadiens 20 minutes away from their 1986 Stanley Cup, an injured Nilan gets lip smacked by The Coach on national television. Anybody else. Anybody. And you just know Knuckles would have cranked him one, but good.

GAME 7

"PATRICK ROY SAVED OUR ASS!"

Many memorable quotes have come our way courtesy of the Canadiens. Players, coaches and the press have all uttered that one phrase that nails a situation bang-on. When Guy Carbonneau stared into the TV cameras and said: "Patrick Roy saved our ass," after the Canadiens were finally bumped by Boston in the 1994 playoffs, everyone knew the score.

Match the hockey men and their words of wisdom.

(Solution is on page 119)

Part 1

John Ferguson	Toe Blake
Sam Pollock	Jean Perron
Ken Dryden	Clarence Campbell

1. _____ "Predictions are for gypsies."

2. _____ "A good businessman cannot be a cheerleader. Cheerleaders don't win anything."

3. _____ "If I could be a forward, I would want to be Bob Gainey.

4. _____ "Me resign?"

5. _____ "The media and the fans are with you win or tie. But don't tie too often."

6. _____ "Without me they would have no one to hate."

Part 2

Guy Lafleur   Frank Selke

Vincent Damphousse   Senator Hartland Molson

Patrick Roy   Punch Imlach

Dick Irvin   Bobby Clarke

1. _____ "Richard may be too brittle to play in the National Hockey League."

2. _____ "Excuses are for losers."

3. _____ "I knew it was early because Rocket Richard had his eyes closed in the picture on the dressing-room wall."

4. _____ "Clean the toilets. This place smells like a pissoir."

5. _____ "Maybe we've overlooked the guys who drive the Zambonis" (on the appointment of Gil Stein to Hall of Fame).

6. _____ "The best player I ever coached" (on Jean Béliveau).

7. _____ "I don't score for myself. I score for the fans."

8. _____ "There are players in this league who make fans out of the rest of us. Lafleur was like that. He was the kind of player you not only played against, but you watched when he was on the ice."

8

THE RECORD HOLDERS

When Scotty Bowman walked into the dressing room before the last game of 1976–77, the Canadiens had 59 wins, an 18-point lead in first place overall and little motivation except to finally be rid of the regular season. His words that night about being the only team in NHL history to win 60 season games pushed his players to establish a league record, one that still stands today. This quiz is devoted to team totals, individual scoring and goalie records.

(Answers are on page 88)

8.1 **Which Canadien holds the team record for most goals in a rookie season?**
A. Maurice Richard
B. Kjell Dahlin
C. Bernie Geoffrion
D. Guy Lafleur

8.2 **Which Canadiens' goalie holds the NHL record for most 40-win seasons?**
A. Jacques Plante
B. Ken Dryden
C. Rogie Vachon
D. Patrick Roy

8.3 **Which Canadien holds the NHL record for fastest Cup-winning goal (from start of the game)?**
A. Mario Tremblay
B. Kirk Muller
C. Jean Béliveau
D. Toe Blake

8.4 Besides Maurice Richard, which other Canadien shares the team record for most points in a game?
A. Elmer Lach
B. Bobby Rousseau
C. Mats Naslund
D. Bert Olmstead

8.5 In what season did Maurice Richard score the NHL's first 50 goals in 50 games?
A. 1942–43
B. 1943–44
C. 1944–45
D. 1945–46

8.6 Which Canadiens' goaltender recorded the most shutouts in one season in league history?
A. Ken Dryden
B. George Hainsworth
C. Georges Vézina
D. Gump Worsley

8.7 Which Canadiens' rookie holds the NHL record for fastest fight from the start of a career?
A. Lou Fontinato
B. John Ferguson
C. Chris Nilan
D. John Kordic

8.8 What is the greatest point-spread margin of defeat suffered by the Canadiens in a modern-day game?
A. Eight goals
B. Nine goals
C. 10 goals
D. 11 goals

8.9 **What ended ex-Canadien Doug Jarvis's ironman streak?**
A. He was scratched from the lineup
B. A freak injury at practice
C. The stalled negotiations of a new contract
D. He retired from hockey

8.10 **Who holds the Canadiens' record for most goals by a player in his first NHL game?**
A. Alex Smart
B. Henri Richard
C. Joe Malone
D. Ralph Backstrom

8.11 **Which Canadiens' player holds the NHL record for fastest penalty shot from the start of the game in regular season play?**
A. Bob Gainey
B. Maurice Richard
C. Brian Skrudland
D. Dickie Moore

8.12 **Which defenseman has scored the most goals in one season?**
A. Serge Savard
B. Larry Robinson
C. Chris Chelios
D. Guy Lapointe

8.13 **The Canadiens hold the NHL record for the highest regular season point total for a non-play-off team. What is the highest number of season points the Canadiens earned while failing to make post-season play?**
A. 80 to 85 points
B. 85 to 90 points
C. 90 to 95 points
D. 95 to 100 points

8.14 Who was the youngest Canadien ever inducted into the NHL Hall of Fame?
A. Yvan Cournoyer
B. Ken Dryden
C. Guy Lafleur
D. Jacques Lemaire

8.15 What NHL playoff record does Maurice Richard still hold single-handedly?
A. Most playoff points in one period
B. Most playoff goals in one game
C. Most playoff game-winning goals in a career
D. Most playoff overtime goals in a career

THE RECORD HOLDERS
Answers

8.1 A & B. Maurice Richard and Kjell Dahlin.
Richard and Guy Lafleur each had the kind of rookie season labelled for the Calder Trophy, except for two remarkable similarities that intervened 28 years apart. Not alike Lafleur's first season in 1971–72 when Ken Dryden and Buffalo rookie Rick Martin amassed the most Calder votes, in 1943–44, Richard's rookie record (32–22–54) was out-inched by Toronto's Gus Bodnar and outclassed by the Habs' new goalie Bill Durnan. In both cases a hotter rookie shooter and a new Habs net-minder snared first and runner-up balloting from these budding Canadiens superstars. No matter, Richard's 32-goal inaugural season remains a club record, equalled only by Dahlin in 1985–86. Drafting him 82nd overall in 1981, the Canadiens waited four years before Dahlin played his first NHL season and then only to see him fizzle out in two short NHL years before returning to Sweden.

CANADIENS TOP ROOKIE GOAL-SCORERS

Player	Season	Games	Goals
1. M. Richard	1943–44	46	32
2. K. Dahlin	1985–86	77	32
3. B. Geoffrion	1951–52	67	30
4. Guy Lafleur	1971–72	73	29
5. Mats Naslund	1982–83	74	26
6. Jacques Lemaire	1967–68	69	22

Current to 1993–94

8.2   A. Jacques Plante.

After playing on six teams (including the WHA Edmonton Oilers!) in his 19-year career, Plante leads all NHL netminders with three 40-or-more-wins seasons, all coming in Vézina Trophy-winning years with the Canadiens: 1955–56 (42 wins), 1959–60 (40 wins) and 1961–62 (42 wins).

8.3   C. Jean Béliveau.

It was a night Forum fans will never forget. Game seven of the 1965 Stanley Cup finals against Bobby Hull's Blackhawks, and the Canadiens leave little doubt about who is the hungriest by popping four goals in period one, the first coming only 14 seconds after the opening faceoff off captain Béliveau's stick. Something was definitely in the Forum air. Call it a pre-victory glow, the ghost of champions past or just a hockey sense about the game's momentum. Gump Worsley stopped everything, including five great saves in the first period to squash any Hawk attack. Canadiens won 4-0 and Béliveau registered the NHL's fastest Cup-winning goal and its first Conn Smythe Trophy performance.

8.4   D. Bert Olmstead.

Richard's highest-scoring game happened on December 28, 1944, the night of the famous eight-point game he almost never played. His near-absence, due to fatigue from moving his family household the previous night, was nixed by coach Dick Irvin, who played Richard on only a few hours' sleep and saw him net five goals and three assists. Ten years later, Olmstead, playing on a line with Richard, tied The Rocket's team mark in an eight-point outing, scoring four goals and four assists against Chicago on January 9, 1954. Their records stand today.

8.5   C. 1944–45.

Bolstered by his Punch Line teammates of Elmer Lach and Toe Blake, Richard tore through the 1944–45 season on a scoring spree the likes of which the NHL had never seen before: 50 goals in 50 games. So remarkable was the Rocket's record that 16 years passed before another 50-goal season was recorded, and that took 62 games. The Rocket spared no one on his way to 50. In Toronto, before a thunderous ovation, he equalled the 28-year-old single-season scoring mark of 44 goals set by the great Joe Malone; one week later he smashed that record in front of a delirious Forum crowd that witnessed Malone himself handing Richard the historic puck that broke his record. In the Canadiens final season game in Boston, the 50th goal was done (with only 2:15 remaining) and the Richard legend set in stone. In an era when 20 goals was like hitting .300 in baseball, the Rocket matched Babe Ruth's pinnacle of 60 home runs. Richard's standard of offensive excellence is still the measure for today's best.

8.6   B. George Hainsworth.

1928–29 was known as "the year of the shutout." Little wonder! In the 44-game schedule, 11 goaltenders notched 120 shutouts and Hainsworth had 22 of them, a remarkable record no netminder has approached (next closest is Tony Esposito's 15 SOs in 1969–70). But not all of the Hainsworth's shutouts were Canadiens wins. Why not? Six of the 22 shutouts were scoreless ties, 0–0.

8.7   B. John Ferguson.
Ferguson came to the Canadiens with one intent: to be the toughest player in the NHL. Hired by GM Sam Pollock to protect his star forwards, Ferguson wasted little time in fulfilling his mandate. Only 12 seconds after the puck was dropped in his first game (October 8, 1963), Ferguson was pummelling Boston tough guy Ted Green. All at once, the Canadiens had more skating room and a new heavyweight to keep the peace. If that wasn't enough, Ferguson scored two goals that night.

8.8   C. 10 goals.
When the Canadiens got trashed 9–0 by Detroit on April 13, 1994, they weren't intentionally aiming to break any records. But they came close, to within one goal-against of a team record 10–0. That double-digit loss, also to the Red Wings, on January 4, 1942 is the Canadiens' worst margin of defeat ever. A couple of soft goals from 40 and 50 feet out helped the loser's ill-fated cause.

8.9   A. He was scratched from the lineup.
The ironman streak ended in Boston on October 11, 1987 while Jarvis was playing for Hartford. After four Canadiens' Cups, the Selke Trophy as top defensive forward, the Bill Masterton Trophy for dedication to hockey and 12 straight, complete 80-game seasons plus two games to open 1987–88, Jarvis, 32, got the word from coach Jack Evans and sat out his first game since his days as a 19-year-old junior in Peterborough. 964 consecutive NHL games later, a club record 560 as a Canadien, Jarvis and the Boston Garden crowd heard:

"Scratch No. 27, Doug Jarvis." He never played in the NHL again. (FYI: Jarvis had become the NHL's iron man, breaking Garry Unger's old record of 914 games on December 26, 1986. The game was played against, you guessed it, the Canadiens.)

8.10   A. Alex Smart.
The Brandon, Manitoba, native managed only eight games in his brief NHL career but set two Canadiens records and one NHL record on January 14, 1943 when he scored three goals in a four-point night, awarding him most goals and most points by a player in his first NHL game. Smart is tied with the Nordiques' Réal Cloutier for the league record in the most goals category.

8.11   B. Maurice Richard.
Arguably, the one and only NHL record The Rocket still holds in regular season is his penalty shot goal which happened 12 seconds into play against Chicago's Harry Lumley on January 1, 1952. Oddly enough, officials ruled Jim Peters of the 'Hawks hooked, not Richard, but Bert Olmstead from behind, yet the shot was awarded to the Rocket (presumably because Olmstead was injured after being pulled down on the play). Montréal defeated the Hawks 3–0, giving Richard the second fastest game winner in NHL history.

8.12   D. Guy Lapointe.
In his fifth full season with the Canadiens, Lapointe set a team record, notching 28 goals in 1974–75. Defensemate Savard potted 20 goals that season, producing the first NHL team in history with two 20-goal scorers on defense in the same season. Lapointe also holds a club record 15 goals for a rookie defenseman.

8.13 C. 90 to 95 points.

Since 1948 the Canadiens have missed the playoffs only once. And in 1969–70 when they finished fifth with 92 points it set an NHL record for highest point total for a non-playoff team. In fact, the Canadiens and the Rangers had identical wins, losses and ties that season. But New York finished with a better record in season goals-for; two up on the Canadiens. To deepen the wound, 92 points (or fifth spot in the East Division) was six points better than first place St. Louis in the West Division.

8.14 B. Ken Dryden.

When Dryden was elected into the Hall of Fame in 1983 he was 35 years, 11 months old, the youngest Canadien inductee but closely followed by Lafleur (36 years, 10 months) in 1988, Cournoyer (38 years, 9 months) in 1982 and Lemaire (38 years, 10 months) in 1984.

8.15 D. Most playoff overtime goals in a career.

In Richard's era, Cup winners could sweep their opponents in two rounds by winning a minimum eight games in less than two weeks. Today's playoff format stretches two months and four rounds, long enough to give the Gretzkys, Lemieuxs and Bossys plenty of Richard records to break. Yet, 35 years since his retirement, the name Maurice Richard still dots the playoff books. The Rocket is tied in a number of categories (A, B & C) but alone holds the playoff career overtime mark with six goals, easily out-distancing Wayne Gretzky, Dale Hunter, Glenn Anderson and Bobby Nystrom, who each have four. Three of Richard's tallies came in 1951, tying the mark first set by Mel Hill in 1939. Richard's other three overtime goals were all scored in years (1946, 1957 and 1958) when the Habs won the Cup.

Across

1. Most Hab goals/one game
2. Lafleur's 1st yr. 19__
4. Fastest OT goal/Skrudland
5. Plante SO total
7. Most losses one year
8. Lapointe's total points
11. Coach Irvin $ fine for being late at practice
12. Cournoyer's uniform No.___
13. Yr. Burns replaced Perron
15. Dryden SO total
16. Robinson's goal totals
18. No. games Rocket played
20. Yr. Lafleur retired again
22. Shutt's uniform No.
23. Usual goalie uniform No.
24. Age Rocket hit 50-in-50
25. Béliveau goal totals
26. Robinson's point totals
28. Most season pts. by defenseman
29. Rocket's goal totals
31. Official Forum capacity
35. Games Lafleur used/1000 pts.
37. Yr. of 23rd Cup
39. Big Bird's uniform No.
40. No. games Cournoyer played
42. Mario Tremblay's goal totals
43. Béliveau's first deal in $
45. Most season pts. by Habs
46. Harvey's assist totals
48. '93's playoff overtime run
49. Lafleur's total goals w. Habs
52. Claude Lemieux's uniform No.
54. Morenz's goal total
56. Savard's game totals
57. Robinson's assist totals
58. Little M's uniform No.
59. Rocket's magic season total
60. Nilan's uniform No.
61. Games Boomer used/50 Goal/yr.
63. Most pts./all Habs one yr.
65. Standing room at Forum
66. Plante's game totals
67. Yr. Richard's 50-in-50

Down

1. Yr. of Richard Riot
3. Provost's game totals
6. Shutt's game totals
7. Cournoyer's goal total
9. Habs record/most career PIMs by Nilan
10. Lafleur's last Art Ross yr.
13. Habs last Cup yr.
14. First yr. of Habs radio broadcast
16. Béliveau's game totals
17. Most goals scored/one season
19. Lafleur's assist totals
21. Béliveau's 1st cheque for his foundation, in $
27. Habs record/most season PIMs by Nilan
28. Habs record/most season assists
30. Lemaire's assist totals
32. Naslund's total points
33. Yr. Rocket breaks Stewart's all-time goal record
34. Yr. Dryden wins rookie of year
35. Talbot's game totals
36. No. of seats in Forum in 1940s
37. Yr. Dryden articles in Toronto
38. Desjardins's uniform No.
41. Habs record/most assists by defenseman/Robinson
43. Habs record/Henri's game totals
44. Habs record/most goals by player one season
45. Béliveau's game totals
47. Habs record/Lafleur's pt. total
48. Béliveau's 1st yr. salary
50. Harvey's game totals
51. Shutt's point totals
53. Rocket's PIM totals
55. Gainey's point totals
57. Henri's assists totals
60. Naslund's assist totals
62. Little M's goal totals
63. Lafleur's uniform No.
64. Rocket's hat trick totals

GAME 8
CROSSNUMBER: PLAYING BY THE NUMBERS

(Solution is on page 119)

9

SHOOTOUTS

Before we head into post-season action and the Stanley Cup chapter, we take a break from multiple choice to test your stamina on a wide variety of subjects in the true or false category. How well you do here could be determined by how closely you've paid attention to facts from previous chapters.

(Answers are on page 98)

9.1   **Toe Blake won 11 Stanley Cups with the Canadiens. T or F?**

9.2   **Marcel Dionne was playing NHL hockey before brother Gilbert Dionne was born. T or F?**

9.3   **Canadiens management traded both superstars Howie Morenz and Georges Vézina in their careers. T or F?**

9.4   **Jacques Plante never won the Vézina Trophy without Doug Harvey on defense. T or F?**

9.5   **Since its inception in 1925 only two Canadiens' players have been awarded the Lady Byng Trophy for gentlemanly conduct. T or F?**

9.6   **Bernie Geoffrion recorded the NHL's second 50-goal season only after Maurice Richard retired. T or F?**

9.7   **Patrick Roy and Guy Lafleur played in only one game together as members of the Montréal Canadiens. T or F?**

9.8 Guy Lafleur retired after Steve Shutt was traded. T or F?

9.9 The first goal scored at the Montréal Forum was by a player who wore jersey No. 13. T or F?

9.10 Larry Robinson is the only Canadien defenseman to wear No. 19 and get traded to Los Angeles. T or F?

9.11 The Canadiens once skated off the ice before the customary handshakes in a Stanley Cup final game. T or F?

9.12 Jean Béliveau never scored an NHL overtime goal. T or F?

9.13 John Ferguson never played in an NHL All-Star Game. T or F?

9.14 Henri Richard won five Stanley Cups in his first five years in the NHL. T or F?

9.15 Vladislav Tretiak was the first Soviet drafted by the Montréal Canadiens. T or F?

9.16 At least one Canadien has had a five-goal game in each of the decades since the team's founding in 1910. T or F?

9.17 Jean Béliveau has the most penalty minutes of any Art Ross Trophy winner in NHL history. T or F?

9.18 Guy Lafleur was almost traded to Buffalo for Gilbert Perreault. T or F?

9.19 On penalty shots, Patrick Roy stops the puck more often than shooters score. T or F?

9.20 Ken Dryden is the only player in NHL history ever to win a major individual award before winning the Calder Trophy as rookie of the year. T or F?

9.21 John Ferguson was once offered the captaincy of the Canadiens. T or F?

9.22 Guy Lafleur reached the 50-goal mark before Pierre Larouche when they each scored 50 goals as teammates on the Canadiens in 1979–80. T or F?

SHOOTOUTS
Answers

9.1 **False.**
Blake did win 11 Cups, but his first championship, 1935, came as a raw rookie winger with the Montréal Maroons and not the Canadiens. The following season Blake was sent "across the street" to the Canadiens and in 1938, the year the Maroons folded, he caught fire and won the Art Ross and Hart Trophies as the league's leading scorer and its most valuable player. After winning the Maroons' Cup in 1935, another nine years passed before Blake sipped champagne again. Of course, he made up it with 10 more Canadiens Cups in the years to come.

9.2 **False.**
19 years separate brothers Gilbert and Marcel Dionne. When the elder stepped onto Detroit ice for his first shift in 1971, younger brother Gilbert was taking his

first steps as a one-year-old in Drummondville, Québec.

9.3 False.
The Canadiens have traded away their superstars, and Morenz was one of them, dealt in 1934 to Chicago. In return the Habs picked up Roger Jenkins and Leroy Goldsworthy. Vézina played his entire career with the Canadiens.

9.4 False.
As great as Harvey was, and as important his loss, the Canadiens still finished first in 1961–62 behind the net-minding of Plante, who proved that winning the Vézina wasn't conditional on the defensive skills of his ex-teammate. It was Plante's sixth Vézina in seven seasons. He would win another (with Glenn Hall in St. Louis) in 1968–69. On defense that year was a guy named Doug Harvey.

9.5 True.
Until Mats Naslund won it in 1988, the last (and only other) Lady Byng winner from the Canadiens' ranks was Toe Blake, a surprise candidate who, despite his tough competitive nature, registered just one 2-minute penalty (against Doug Bentley) in 1945–46.

9.6 True.
After being loudly booed and abused by Forum fans for winning the scoring race against their beloved hero, Maurice Richard, in 1955, it's almost too coincidental that Geoffrion waited until The Rocket retired to equal his 50-goal record. On that night, March 16, 1961, Geoffrion's standing ovation signalled his return to the hearts of all Canadiens fans.

9.7 False.

In Lafleur's year of retirement, 1984–85, Roy played only 20 minutes of hockey, too late for The Flower who retired just 19 games into the season. In later years, they did challenge each other several times during Lafleur's comeback with New York and Québec.

9.8 True.

Eight days after the Shutt trade (18/11/84) to Los Angeles, Lafleur announced his retirement (26/11/84) from the Canadiens.

9.9 True.

Billy Boucher, the Canadiens only No. 13 ever, scored the Forum's very first goal on November 29, 1924.

9.10 False.

The other No. 19 Canadien defenseman involved in a Kings trade was Terry Harper. He was dealt in 1972, a year before Robinson joined the Habs.

9.11 True.

After fighting back from a 3–1 series deficit to be deadlocked 1–1 in seventh game overtime with their archrivals the Red Wings, the Canadiens lose the 1954 Cup on a fluke goal, deflected in off of Doug Harvey's glove. A whole year's work blown on a garbage goal by the much-hated Wings. The bitterness was too much. The Canadiens skate off Detroit ice without congratulating their opponents.

9.12 False.

In 162 playoff games over 18 seasons, Béliveau scored just one overtime winner. It came on April 24th, 1969 at the 11:28 mark of the second overtime period in game six of the semi-finals against Boston's Gerry Cheevers.

9.13 False.
Yes, Ferguson laced up with the Howes, Hulls and Mikitas to play all star hockey, but his accomplishment is only tainted by the fact that his invitation came when the game's format called for the defending Stanley Cup winners to play the league's best. No matter, Ferguson attended not once but twice (1965 and 1967) and even scored two goals in the Canadiens' 3–0 shutout against the All Stars in 1967.

9.14 True.
Richard's first five years coincided with the Canadiens setting the NHL's all-time consecutive record for championships—five Cups from 1956 to 1960.

9.15 False.
Tretiak, 138th overall in 1983, was drafted five years after Viacheslav Fetisov, the Canadiens' first-ever Soviet pick (201st overall) from 1978. Neither ever played for the Canadiens.

9.16 False.
Excluding the 1990s, the only decade since 1910 that hasn't produced a five-goal game scorer is the 1980s.

9.17 False.
Béliveau's 1955–56 totals of 47 goals and 88 points guaranteed the Art Ross Trophy, but his 143 penalty minutes that year also made him the NHL's most penalized scoring leader. That hollow distinction was erased by Stan Mikita whose scoring title year of 1963–64 produced 146 penalty minutes, three minutes better than Béliveau's totals.

9.18 True.
In any conceivable Lafleur trade, the only NHLer remotely acceptable to Montréal fans might have been Perreault. Irving Grundman knew it when talks were

initiated with Sabres' lawyer Bob Swados at a governor's meeting in 1982. But the deal never materialized (after Perreault settled his contract dispute with Buffalo), leaving one to wonder what might have been.

9.19 False.
Although NHL goalies have a 55.8% success rate to shooters' 44.2%, Roy has bucked that trend in five one-on-one match-ups since 1985, stopping only one penalty shot, his first (January 1, 1986), while shooters have succeeded in their last four attempts.

9.20 True.
With only six regular season game behind him, Dryden stepped into the breach of the 1971 playoffs and came out the Conn Smythe winner as MVP, a full season before he won the NHL's top rookie award in 1972.

9.21 True.
In 1971, when Jean Béliveau and Ferguson retired, GM Sam Pollock asked the Canadiens' enforcer to reconsider and play another season, this time as team captain. Not too many players have turned down an offer to wear the "C" for the Canadiens. But Fergie did, recognizing Pollock's gesture as thanks for his invaluable contribution to team leadership.

9.22 False.
Larouche and Lafleur each scored exactly 50 goals in 1979-80, only the second time the Canadiens have had two 50-goal scorers in one season. They both did it in their 72nd game. Larouche hit the 50-goal mark first against Chicago's Tony Esposito on March 25, 1980, while Lafleur followed up three games later popping his 50th on April 2, 1980 against Detroit's Rogie Vachon.

CUP WINNERS

In 24 Stanley Cups, 19 Canadiens players have scored Cup-winning goals. Match the famous goal-scorers below and the championship year they notched the winner.

(Solution is on page 120)

Jean Béliveau   Jacques Lemaire
Toe Blake   Dickie Moore
Marcel Bonin   Howie Morenz
Yvan Cournoyer   Kirk Muller
John Ferguson   Henri Richard
Johnny Gagnon   Maurice Richard
Bernie Geoffrion   Bobby Smith
Elmer Lach   J.-C. Tremblay
Guy Lafleur   Mario Tremblay

1916	G. Prodgers	1924 & 30	_____
1931	_____	1944 & 46	_____
1953	_____	1956	_____
1957	_____	1958	_____
1959	Marcel Bonin	1960 & 65	_____
1966 & 71	Henri Richard	1968	_____
1969	John Ferguson	1973	_____
1976	Guy Lafleur	1977 & 79	_____
1978	Mario Tremblay	1986	_____
1993	Kirk Muller		

10

TWENTY-FOUR AND COUNTING . . .

The Stanley Cup is engraved with the names of almost two hundred Canadiens who have played on 24 championships since 1915. No other NHL club can claim so many champions as the Montréal Canadiens. No other NHL rink but the Forum holds as many Cup banners or has seen as many on-ice celebrations. And no city has honoured its team with parades as frequently as Montréal. In this chapter we're goin' to The Show, hockey's highest honour and one of sport's longest-standing traditions.

(Answers are on page 108)

10.1 **Who did the Montréal Canadiens defeat to win their first Stanley Cup?**
A. The Portland Rosebuds
B. The Québec Bulldogs
C. The Vancouver Millionaires
D. The Montréal Wanderers

10.2 **What was the most frequent final score when the Canadiens won a record 10 straight overtime playoff games en route to 1993's Stanley Cup?**
A. 2–1
B. 3–2
C. 4–3
D. 5–4

10.3 Why didn't Larry Robinson's overtime goal count in the 1979 Rangers–Canadiens finals?
A. Because of a high stick and a late offside whistle
B. Because the referee didn't see the puck go in the net
C. Because of a Canadiens scramble inside the crease
D. Because the referee ruled the puck was gloved in

10.4 The second youngest player ever to score a Stanley Cup winning goal was a member of the Montréal Canadiens. Who was he?
A. John Ferguson
B. Yvan Cournoyer
C. Mario Tremblay
D. Bobby Smith

10.5 Who scored the overtime goal that eliminated Boston in game seven of the 1979 semi-finals?
A. Guy Lafleur
B. Larry Robinson
C. Yvon Lambert
D. Serge Savard

10.6. When the Canadiens won five straight Stanley Cups between 1956 and 1960, they could have played a maximum of 70 playoff games over 10 series, two series per year in the best-of-seven format. How many playoff games did they lose during their drive-for-five?
A. Between zero and five games
B. Between five and 10 games
C. Between 10 and 15 games
D. More than 15

10.7 How many times have the Canadiens reached the Stanley Cup finals, only to lose?
A. Only once, in 1988–89
B. Two to five times
C. Six to 10 times
D. More than 10 times

10.8 In the Canadiens' famous 7–5 comeback game against the Bruins in the 1971 semi-finals, who scored the game winner?
A. Henri Richard
B. Jean Béliveau
C. John Ferguson
D. Yvan Cournoyer

10.9 What prevented the Canadiens and Seattle Metropolitans from finishing the 1919 Stanley Cup finals?
A. A severe earthquake
B. An influenza epidemic
C. A train crash
D. Unseasonably warm weather

10.10 In what post-season year between 1956 and 1960 did the Canadiens eliminate the opposition in the fewest number of games?
A. 1956
B. 1957
C. 1959
D. 1960

10.11 Among the many escapades endured over the years by the Stanley Cup (i.e., drop-kicked into the Rideau Canal; submerged in Mario Lemieux's swimming pool), one of the most famous incidents involved some Canadiens' champions. Which players forgot the Cup on a Montréal street for several hours?
A. Sprague Cleghorn and Georges Vézina
B. Doug Harvey and Floyd Curry
C. Guy Lafleur and Serge Savard
D. Mario Tremblay and Chris Chelios

10.12 What is the longest the Canadiens have gone without winning the Stanley Cup?
A. No more than six seasons
B. Seven to nine seasons
C. 10 to 12 seasons
D. More than 12 seasons

10.13 What did Patrick Roy do during the on-ice celebrations after winning the 1993 Stanley Cup?
A. He checked his name engraved on the Cup in 1986.
B. He called out a sponsor's name.
C. He autographed his stick for Gary Bettman.
D. He dropped the Cup.

10.14 Which Stanley Cup-winning team had the most rookies?
A. The 1955–56 Canadiens
B. The 1964–65 Canadiens
C. The 1972–73 Canadiens
D. The 1985–86 Canadiens

10.15 What player scored the turn-around goal in game seven of the 1971 Cup finals with the Canadiens trailing Chicago 2–0?
A. Jean Béliveau
B. Henri Richard
C. Jacques Lemaire
D. Guy Lapointe

10.16 What special word is inscribed on the Canadiens 1992–93 Stanley Cup rings?
A. "Always"
B. "Glorieux"
C. "Together"
D. "Victory"

TWENTY-FOUR AND COUNTING
Answers

10.1 **A. The Portland Rosebuds.**
In 1916, when the Rosebuds arrived in Montréal to play the Canadiens for the best-of-five final, the Stanley Cup was still a challenge trophy played between the western champions of the PCHA (Pacific Coast Hockey Association), Portland, and their eastern NHA (National Hockey Association) counterparts, the Canadiens. It was Montréal's first ever Cup final. And a classic, witnessed by small but boisterous crowds and played on the natural ice surface of Jubilee Rink. Game one was won 2–0 by the train-weary Rosebuds, but Canadiens stars like Newsy Lalonde, Jack Laviolette and Georges Vézina took the series lead with back-to-back wins, only marred by a brawl which, according to the *Gazette*, "was not brought to a finish until police chief Moffatt and his constables forced their way onto the ice and laid a warning hand on the combatants."

Portland came back 6–5 in game four to set up the deciding match on March 30, 1916. With four minutes remaining, the score tied 1–1, former Québec Bulldog Goldie Prodgers broke Portland with a tough end-to-end rush to pot the winner. The Canadiens took seven years to win their first Stanley Cup. On this one occasion, there was no civic parade or celebration (although each player did receive $238 for the victory).

10.2   C. 4–3.

When the Canadiens won an unprecedented 10 straight overtime games they broke more than an NHL record. They shattered the law of averages. Canadiens pushed their luck, winning five overtimes by a 4–3 margin, once each against the Kings and the Islanders and three squeekers in a row to eliminate Buffalo. When the Isles went down in the extra period 4-3, it was their first post-season overtime loss since 1985 after compiling a lifetime 29–7 OT record.

THE CANADIENS' PERFECT 10 OVERTIME DRIVE

Game	Score	OT winner	Time
OT No.1	Habs 2 – Nords 1	Damphousse	10:30
OT No.2	Habs 5 – Nords 4	Muller	8:17
OT No.3	Habs 4 – Sabres 3	Carbonneau	2:50
OT No.4	Habs 4 – Sabres 3	Dionne	8:28
OT No.5	Habs 4 – Sabres 3	Muller	11:37
OT No.6	Habs 4 – Isles 3	Lebeau	26:21
OT No.7	Habs 2 – Isles 1	Carbonneau	12:34
OT No.8	Habs 3 – Kings 2	Desjardins	:51
OT No.9	Habs 4 – Kings 3	LeClair	:34
OT No.10	Habs 3 – Kings 2	LeClair	14:37

10.3 B. Because the referee didn't see the puck go in the net.

In the days before video replay, goal judges and referees were known to miss a penalty or goal on occasion(!). If we've complicated our grand old game, it's so that goals like Robinson's will count in the final score. Tied in overtime against the Rangers, Robinson fires a fast riser, pinging it off the net's inside post and out again before referee Andy Van Hellemond can blink. A minute later at 7:25 into OT Serge Savard scores on a backhander to give the Canadiens their "second" overtime goal, this one counting. Robinson, credited with an overtime "shot on net," retires in 1991–92, coincidentally, the first year the NHL employs video replay.

10.4 C. Mario Tremblay.

Tremblay was 21 years, 8 months old when he wristed home the 1978 Cup winner against Boston's Gerry Cheevers. The goal, assisted by Conn Smythe winner Larry Robinson, came in game six at 9:20 of the first period on May 25, 1978. It was Tremblay's third Stanley Cup in his first four years with the Canadiens. Who was the youngest? Toronto's Ted Kennedy.

10.5 C. Yvon Lambert.

No two NHL teams have battled each other more often or more fiercely at playoff time than Boston and Montréal. It's a tradition born of bitter struggle, built on gritty play, series-winning turnovers and heartbreaking goals by hero all-stars and, finally, fuelled by fine hockey men like Boston GM Harry Sinden, who, with all his faculties intact, could lay blame to more than one Boston loss at the hands of the fabled ghosts of the Forum. To be sure, 1979 proved to be the classic Bruins–Canadiens confrontation that cemented their rivalry in hockey lore forever. It was the year the Canadiens played the final series in the semi-finals; the year, coach Don Cherry stood on the Forum visitors' bench taunting and admonishing Montréal fans with outstretched arms; and it was the year Yvon Lambert broke the Bruins' backs with his overtime goal. It happened on May 10, 1979. Game seven. The Canadiens trailing 3–1 in the third get two power play goals from Guy Lafleur and Mark Napier to tie. Rick Middleton stuffs one in from behind the net: 4–3. With Sinden's Forum ghosts all over the Bruins, Cherry's team is dealt a too-many-men-on-the-ice penalty. Lafleur's big blast sends the team into overtime. Boston never had a chance.

10.6   B. Between five and 10 games.

In five playoff years Montréal played 49 games (of a maximum 70 games), winning 40, losing just nine games. Their playoff record is indicative of the powerhouse GM Frank Selke had assembled and Blake inherited. In only two of 10 series were the Canadiens forced beyond five games, winning another three series four straight.

10.7   C. Six to 10 times.

Since winning their first Cup in 1916, the Canadiens have gone to the Cup finals 34 times in 79 years, losing nine championships (and one no-decision final in 1918–19) to Detroit and Toronto three times each and once to Calgary, Victoria and Seattle. Their most consistent loss record occurred under three-time Cup-winner coach Dick Irvin, who, it was unfairly said, "couldn't win the big one" after losing five Cup finals, four between 1951 and 1955.

10.8   C. John Ferguson.

Béliveau, 40 years old and playing against the Bruins' young turks, was the comeback hero scoring two goals and two assists, one of which fed linemate Ferguson for the game winner at 15:23 of the third period. By that time the game's momentum had long shifted to the Habs, who had been down 5–1 but roared back after a second period Richard goal and three in the third from the Béliveau-Cournoyer-Ferguson line. Jacques Lemaire and Frank Mahovlich also scored in the 7–5 upset which set the Bruins on their heels for the rest of the series, never recovering and missing their chance at a dynasty.

10.9   B. An influenza epidemic.

The only time in Stanley Cup history no champion was declared occurred in 1919 when the Canadiens travelled to Seattle for a best-of-seven final against the Metropolitans. After five games, two wins apiece and a scoreless tie, the series was halted when several players fell ill, including Canadiens' forward Joe Hall, who died, a victim of that year's infamous epidemic of Spanish influenza.

10.10   D. 1960.

The Canadiens won their unprecedented fifth consecutive Stanley Cup in the minimum eight games, defeating Chicago and Toronto in straight sets of four. No other Canadiens' playoff series was so decisive. Jacques Plante, who wore hockey's first goalie mask in post-season action, recorded three shutouts and allowed only five Maple Leaf goals in the finals. Canadiens fans said goodbye to Maurice Richard for the last time. He scored his 34th final-series goal, still an all-time record.

10.11   A. Sprague Cleghorn and Georges Vézina.

With so many Canadiens names engraved on the Cup over the past century of hockey, Stanley has had his share of adventures with Montréal players. Besides the time Guy Lafleur used the Cup as a lawn ornament on his parents' property in Thurso, Québec, one famous story involved Sprague Cleghorn, Georges Vézina and Sylvio Mantha, Canadiens champions of 1924. The post-victory ceremonies took place at owner Léo Dandurand's home in upper Westmount atop Mount Royal. On the way, Dandurand's car failed to make the icy incline of Côte St. Antoine Road. The boys piled out of the boss's Model T, Cleghorn put the Cup on the curb and everyone pushed the car up the hill. Hours later, the celebrations fell silent when it was discovered the Cup was missing. Dandurand and Cleghorn backtracked to the spot where the Model T had initially stalled. Stanley was still sitting there.

10.12 D. More than 12 seasons.

The Canadiens are such consistent winners that they have more than twice as many Stanley Cups as the next closest rival, the Toronto Maple Leafs. Before Frank Selke took over, there were no famous dynasty powerhouses; the Canadiens had won only six Cups prior to 1946, never more frequently than back-to-back championships, and their worst drought lasted 13 years from 1931 to 1944. Selke's farm teams began producing dividends in the way of championships by 1953. Seven years later the Canadiens had doubled their Cup-win record and swept five straight Stanley Cups. Sam Pollock increased the team's winning percentage through trades, draft picks and a hockey/business sense that produced another 10 Cups in 15 seasons.

10.13 B. He called out a sponsor's name.

With Maurice Richard and 17,000 rabid fans cheering them on, the parade of Canadien champions heaved their Cup around the Forum ice, each one in turn arching it over his head as tradition dictates. As Roy skated by a camera, Cup in tow, he yelled: "I'm going to Disney World," plugging the theme park. Before the night was over several more takes were in the can, as

Roy came back onto the ice long after the last reveller had left the stands to correct the English wording for both Disney World and Disneyland.

10.14 D. The 1985–86 Canadiens.

As many as 13 rookies played alongside veterans Bob Gainey, Larry Robinson and Ryan Walter when the Canadiens won the Cup in 1986. It was the first NHL season for Patrick Roy, Claude Lemieux, Stéphane Richer, David Maley, Mike Lalor, Brian Skrudland and others; and only the sophomore year of Chris Chelios, Tom Kurvers, Petr Svoboda and Mike McPhee. Coach Jean Perron was a rookie, too.

10.15 C. Jacques Lemaire.

Lemaire's playoff total is 61 goals, but perhaps his most important goal came in 1971 when he turned the game around by scoring the Canadiens' comeback goal. Ahead 2–0, Chicago's Bobby Hull blasts a slapshot beyond Ken Dryden. It hits the crossbar. Guy Lapointe picks up the rebound and feeds Lemaire who is streaking to centre ice. Lemaire crosses the red line and unleashes a rocket at Tony Esposito. Surprised by the suddenness of the shot, Esposito drops to his usual butterfly position. The puck sails over his shoulder. In those few seconds the Stanley Cup was decided. Had Hull connected, it would have buried the Canadiens 3–0; instead, Lemaire's 70-footer bulged the net and unnerved the Hawks, who never got back in the game, losing 3–2 and handing the Canadiens their 17th Stanley Cup.

10.16 C. "Together."

On the top part of the Canadiens' 14-carat gold championship ring is the profile of the Stanley Cup encrusted with 24 two-point diamonds and surrounded by another set of diamonds. The 24 diamonds commemorate the

Canadiens' 24th Cup; the total diamond weight, one carat or 100 points, represents the 100th anniversary of the Cup. On the sides in high relief are the team name and logo, the player's name and number and the word "Together," an idea courtesy of Jacques Demers.

SOLUTIONS TO GAMES

GAME 1: SWEATER NUMBERS

1. Jacques Plante
2. Doug Harvey
3. Émile Bouchard
4. Jean Béliveau/Aurèle Joliat
5. Guy Lapointe
6. Ralph Backstrom
7. Howie Morenz
8. Dick Duff
9. Maurice Richard
10. Guy Lafleur
11. Kirk Muller
12. Yvan Cournoyer
14. Claude Provost
15. Bobby Rousseau
16. Henri Richard/Elmer Lach

17. John LeClair
18. Serge Savard
19. Larry Robinson
20. Pete Mahovlich
21. Guy Carbonneau
22. Steve Shutt
23. Bob Gainey
24. Chris Chelios
25. Jacques Lemaire
26. Mats Naslund
27. Frank Mahovlich
28. Pierre Larouche
29. Ken Dryden
30. Lorne Worsley
33. Patrick Roy

GAME 2: CROSSWORD: THE HABS

GAME 3: PAST AND FUTURE CONSIDERATIONS

1. J	7. K
2. H	8. D
3. B	9. L
4. I	10. E
5. G	11. F
6. A	12. C

GAME 4: THE ALL-STAR GAME

The leftover letters (in heavy type) spell out in descending order, left to right: 1) D-R-Y-D-E-N, 2) L-E-S G-L-O-R-I-E-U-X and 3) C-A-N-A-D-I-E-N-S

117

GAME 5: THE CAPTAINS

GAME 6: THE WONDER YEARS

1. 1990	6. 1968	11. 1936	16. 1977
2. 1961	7. 1957	12. 1993	17. 1959
3. 1955	8. 1979	13. 1950	18. 1983
4. 1923	9. 1962	14. 1920	19. 1986
5. 1982	10. 1973	15. 1947	20. 1945

GAME 7: "PATRICK ROY SAVED OUR ASS."

Part 1
1. Toe Blake
2. Sam Pollock
3. Ken Dryden
4. Clarence Campbell
   (on the Richard Riot)
5. Jean Perron
6. John Ferguson

Part 2
1. Dick Irvin
2. Patrick Roy
3. Vincent Damphousse
4. Frank Selke
5. Senator Hartland Molson
6. Punch Imlach
7. Guy Lafleur
8. Bobby Clarke

GAME 8: PLAYING BY THE NUMBERS

GAME 9: CUP WINNERS

1916	G. Prodgers	1924-30	H. Morenz
1931	J. Gagnon	1944-46	T. Blake
1953	E. Lach	1956	M. Richard
1957	D. Moore	1958	B. Geoffrion
1959	M. Bonin	1960-65	J. Béliveau
1966-71	H. Richard	1968	J.-C. Tremblay
1969	J. Ferguson	1973	Y. Cournoyer
1976	G. Lafleur	1977-79	J. Lemaire
1978	M. Tremblay	1986	B. Smith
1993	K. Muller		

ACKNOWLEDGEMENTS

The following publishers and organizations have given permission for use of quoted material.

From *The Gazette*. Copyright © 1916. Printed and published in Montreal by Southam Inc. Reprinted by permission of *The Gazette*. From *Lions in Winter*. Copyright © 1994 by Chrys Goyens and Allan Turowetz. Reprinted by permission of McGraw-Hill Ryerson. From *The Trail of the Stanley Cup*. Copyright © 1964 by Charles L. Coleman. From "Hockey World," a CFCF–12 Montreal Production. Copyright © 1993 by CFCF Inc.

SELECT BIBLIOGRAPHY

Coleman, Charles L. *The Trail of the Stanley Cup*. 3 vols. Montréal: National Hockey League, 1976.

Dryden, Ken. *The Game*. Toronto: Macmillan of Canada, 1983.

Germain, Georges-Hébert. *Overtime: The Legend of Guy Lafleur*. Montréal: Art Global/Libre Expression, 1990.

Goyens, Chrys, and Turowetz, Allan. *Lions in Winter*. Toronto: McGraw-Hill Ryerson, 1994.

Hollander, Zander. *The Complete Encyclopedia of Hockey*. Detroit: Visible Ink Press, 1993.

Irvin, Dick. *The Habs*. Toronto: McClelland & Stewart, 1991.

Irvin, Dick. *Now Back To You, Dick*. Toronto: McClelland & Stewart, 1988.

MacGregor, Roy. *Road Games*. Toronto: Macfarlane Walter & Ross, 1993.

McKinley, Michael. *Hockey Hall of Fame Legends*. Toronto: Viking, 1993.

Mouton, Claude. *The Montreal Canadiens*. Toronto: Van Nostrand Reinhold, 1980.

O'Brien, Andy. *Rocket Richard*. Toronto: The Ryerson Press, 1961.

Selke, Frank J. *Behind the Cheering*. Toronto: McClelland & Stewart, 1962.